Blockchain and Robotic Process Automation

Agnes Koschmider • Stefan Schulte

Editors

Blockchain and Robotic Process Automation

 Springer

Editors
Agnes Koschmider (iD)
Kiel University
Kiel, Germany

Stefan Schulte
Hamburg University of Technology
Hamburg, Germany

ISBN 978-3-030-81408-3   ISBN 978-3-030-81409-0   (eBook)
https://doi.org/10.1007/978-3-030-81409-0

This Springer imprint is published by the registered company Springer Nature Switzerland AG.
The registered company address is: Gewerbestrasse 11, 6330 Cham, Switzerland

Preface

Blockchain technologies have gained much attention from both the industry and the research community in recent years. Originally, the large interest could be traced back to the increase of prices of cryptocurrencies like Bitcoin and Ether and related discussions in the media. But today, blockchain technologies and other Distributed Ledger Technologies (DLTs) are not discussed only because of their basic functionality as means for payments. Especially the introduction of smart contracts in second-generation blockchains like Ethereum and Hyperledger has opened myriad possibilities for the application of DLTs in many different areas, e.g., healthcare, the Internet of Things (IoT), and Business Process Management. As a consequence, many different DLTs have been proposed, and thousands of researchers are working on the application of DLTs in new use case areas as well as the further development of DLTs in so different areas like enhanced cryptography, quantum resistance, or interoperability.

This book integrates the material of the lecture series "Blockchain and Robotic Process Automation" offered at Kiel University. The lecture series sheds light on current research topics on blockchain and Robotic Process Automation (RPA) also in combination with Business Process Management (BPM) or process mining. Leading scientists and business experts give insights into the use of the blockchain technology and RPA. The slides and recordings of the lecture series are available online.[1]

The chapters were written by the following experts:

1. Introduction and Background: Blockchain and Smart Contracts (Ingo Weber)
2. Extraction of Meaningful Events for Process Mining from Blockchain (Agnes Koschmider and Frank Duchmann)
3. Challenges of Blockchain-Based Collaborative Business Processes: An Overview of the Caterpillar System (Orlenys López Pintado)
4. Executing DMN Decisions on the Blockchain (Stephan Haarmann)

---

[1] https://deich.pa.informatik.uni-kiel.de/vorlesungBlockchain/.

5. Dimo—Blockchain-Based Solution for Digital Payment (Florian Protschka)
6. Blockchain Use Cases in Transportation and Logistics (Michael Kuperberg and Sviatoslav Butskyi)
7. Automatically Identifying Process Automation Candidates Using Natural Language Processing (Han van der Aa and Henrik Leopold)

We hope you enjoy reading the book,

Kiel, Germany   Agnes Koschmider
Hamburg, Germany   Stefan Schulte
May 2021

Contents

1 Introduction and Background: Blockchain and Smart Contracts 1
Ingo Weber

2 Extraction of Meaningful Events for Process Mining
from Blockchain.. 13
Agnes Koschmider and Frank Duchmann

3 Challenges of Blockchain-Based Collaborative Business
Processes: An Overview of the Caterpillar System........................ 31
Orlenys López Pintado

4 Executing DMN Decisions on the Blockchain 43
Stephan Haarmann

5 Dimo: Blockchain-Based Solution for Digital Payment................... 55
Florian Protschka

6 Blockchain Use Cases in Transportation and Logistics................... 61
Michael Kuperberg and Sviatoslav Butskyi

7 Automatically Identifying Process Automation Candidates
Using Natural Language Processing 77
Han van der Aa and Henrik Leopold

Acronyms

BC4A	Blockchain for Aviation
BCPaaS	Blockchain Platforms-as-a-Service
BIM	Building Information Modeling
BiTA	Blockchain in Transport Alliance
BPM	Business Process Management
BPMN	Business Process Model and Notation
BPMS	Business Process Management System
Cat XoL	Catastrophe Excess of Loss
CIM	Uniform Rules Concerning the Contract of International Carriage of Goods by Rail
dApp	Decentralized Application
DLT	Distributed Ledger Technology
DMN	Decision Model and Notation
DUST	Diamond Unclonable Secure Tag
ERP	Enterprise Resource Planning
IoT	Internet of Things
MaaS	Mobility-as-a-Service
NLP	Natural Language Processing
OBU	On-Board Unit
RPA	Robotic Process Automation
SCM	Supply Chain Management
SMGS	Agreement on International Goods Transport by Rail
SSI	Self-Sovereign Identity
SVM	Support Vector Machine
TCC	Tokenized Carbon Credit
V2G	Vehicle-to-Grid
V2X	Vehicle-to-Everything

Chapter 1
Introduction and Background: Blockchain and Smart Contracts

Ingo Weber

Abstract This chapter introduces blockchain and Distributed Ledger Technologies (DLTs), smart contracts, and how they work. The relevance of these technologies will be discussed in brief for a set of use cases. DLT, blockchain, and smart contracts allow building a distinct set of applications, which we refer to as blockchain-based applications. For such applications, we will discuss the main architectural concerns, including processes for assessing the suitability of blockchain and for designing blockchain-based applications, what to handle on-chain and what to keep off-chain, as well as the main characteristics of blockchain as a base technology. Finally, we will give an overview of architectural design patterns for blockchain-based applications.

1.1 Why Blockchain and DLT, and What Is It?

Computing, digitization, and digital transformation owe their very broad success in part to the feature that digital access to files and resources can be multiplied and parallelized—in simple terms, that computer files can be copied and transferred. Before the introduction of computer systems in workplaces, files were paper-based, and therefore by necessity at exactly one location. Copies could be made and mailed, but synchronizing changes on copies of paper files was hard and often avoided by having just one authoritative version of a file. When files had to be transferred between employees, they had to be carried from one desk to another. With the introduction of computer systems, files could be accessed from multiple desks simultaneously. Copying files became very cheap, and sending files over networks became easy enough not much later.

However, with digital currencies like Bitcoin or Ether, the feature that copying is simple poses a big challenge: how to create a digital equivalent of a coin, such that

I. Weber (✉)
Chair for Software and Business Engineering, TU Berlin, Berlin, Germany
e-mail: ingo.weber@tu-berlin.de

© The Author(s), under exclusive license to Springer Nature Switzerland AG 2021
A. Koschmider, S. Schulte (eds.), *Blockchain and Robotic Process Automation*,
https://doi.org/10.1007/978-3-030-81409-0_1

forgery is hard? If you have a digital coin and can copy it easily, then nobody would assign any value to it. In the basic case, this is the issue of *double-spending*: for a digital currency, no user should be able to spend a coin more than once. This can be ensured in a centralized system: imagine a database, where each "coin" has exactly one owner, and the amount of coins is finite; transferring a coin from one person to another can be set up to ensure that no "copies" are made.

Bitcoin [10] is an example for a digital cryptocurrency which solves this problem in the decentralized case: coins cannot be double-spent, and new coins can only be created in a well-defined way. This cryptocurrency operates on a leader-less peer-to-peer system, and at its core is *blockchain* as the underlying technology. Blockchain has been introduced with Bitcoin (although the term was not publicized initially). It has emerged as a clever combination of concepts from distributed computing, peer-to-peer networking, cryptography, and game theory and incentive systems. But what is it?

To answer that question, we rely on the definitions from Xu et al. [19] in the following. We start with the term "Distributed ledger":

A *Distributed Ledger* is an append-only store of transactions which is distributed across many machines.

The unit of data here is transactions, which, in the simplest case of cryptocurrencies, transfer funds from one account to another account. Typically, data can be attached to a transaction, much like the reference field of a wire transfer. "Append-only" means that new transactions can be added to the end of the ledger, but previous transactions cannot be removed (without very high effort, i.e., high costs).

On this basis, we define blockchain conceptually:

A *blockchain* is a distributed ledger that is structured into a linked list of blocks. Each block contains an ordered set of transactions. Typical solutions use cryptographic hashes to secure the link from a block to its predecessor.

This is depicted in Fig. 1.1. Transactions are now grouped into blocks, and the blocks form a linked list because each block contains the hash of the respective previous block. Within the blocks, transactions are ordered. As a result, we obtain a total order of transactions across all blocks. Due to the use of cryptographic hashes, the blockchain data structure is tamper-evident: if anyone changes any part of a block, e.g., a transaction contained in it, the hash value changes. Therefore, the hash

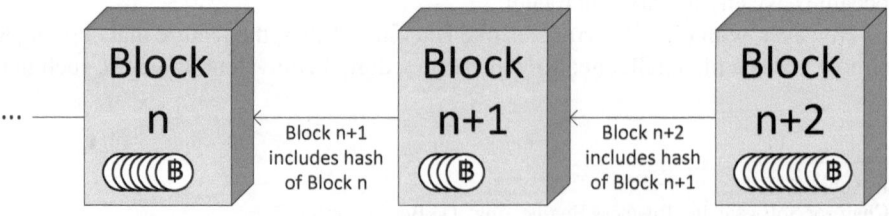

Fig. 1.1 Conceptual view of a blockchain data structure (source: [19])

stored in the next block does not match anymore. Say, the 100th block has been changed; then, in order to re-establish the links, we have to change the hash value stored in block 101. But doing so changes block 101, and therefore its hash value, so the stored hash value in block 102 no longer matches it. In other words, changing any block is either detected as tampering or requires overwriting all subsequent blocks. Given that a blockchain is an append-only ledger, rewriting blocks is typically prevented for any blocks and transactions that are seen as *committed*, i.e., should no longer be changed. Depending on the specific blockchain/DLT, and in some cases even depending on the individual user, the notion of commitment changes.

How to interact on the basis of a blockchain data structure is defined for a blockchain system, which consists of:

- a *blockchain network* of machines, also called *nodes*;
- a blockchain data structure, for the ledger that is replicated across the blockchain network. Nodes that hold a full replica of this ledger are referred to as *full nodes*;
- a *network protocol* that defines rights, responsibilities, and means of communication, verification, validation, and consensus across the nodes in the network. This includes ensuring authorization and authentication of new transactions, mechanisms for appending new blocks, incentive mechanisms (if needed), and similar aspects.

The blockchain network is a peer-to-peer network of machines, across which (part of) the ledger is distributed. The network protocol regulates how these machines interact and who is allowed to do what. The nodes typically do not trust each other and validate each piece of data received, including all transactions and blocks. In Bitcoin (and other cryptocurrencies following similar principles), double-spending is prevented because each "coin" is only allowed to be spent once, and this is verified by each node. Due to the total order of transactions, there can be no concurrent spending of coins in multiple transactions: the transactions are always forced into a total order, and if a "coin" has already been spent in a previous transaction, the second transaction where the same owner tries to spend it is rejected.

In the book [19], we also define *public blockchain* as a specific type of blockchain system, as well as *blockchain platform* as the technology platform used to operate a blockchain system, i.e., the programs running on the nodes (including miners, which are nodes that create new blocks, and wallets through which users have control over their blockchain accounts).

1.2   Smart Contracts: User-Defined Programs on Blockchain

Bitcoin and its underlying blockchain technology are very interesting intellectually, and occasionally also practically, but the use cases requiring "Internet money" that is independent of central banks are rather limited. The interest in blockchain rose dramatically with the introduction of so-called smart contracts in Ethereum, defined in [19] as follows:

> *Smart contracts* are programs deployed as data in the blockchain ledger, and executed in transactions on the blockchain. Smart contracts can hold and transfer digital assets managed by the blockchain, and can invoke other smart contracts stored on the blockchain. Smart contract code is deterministic and immutable once deployed.

The term is arguably misleading: smart contracts are not necessarily smart nor do they typically represent legal contracts—though they *can* be both. The better mental model is that of user-defined programs running on a blockchain system. Using the data fields of transactions, code is deployed on a smart contract-enabled blockchain system (with a special convention of how such transactions are to be interpreted). Once deployed, the functions exposed by the program can be called in other transactions, typically by specifying which deployed contract to call as the recipient of the transaction, and the data field populated with data that specifies which function to call with which parameter values. In order to be reasonably certain about the outcomes of a function call, the code is deterministic with respect to the state of the blockchain and the input parameters. However, the state of the blockchain may change between preparing the transaction and it becoming effective, thus limiting the degree of determinism. Given that a smart contract is deployed by a transaction, and transactions in a blockchain are only appended (and never updated or deleted once committed), any committed deployment transaction renders the smart contract code immutable. More flexibility can be gained by dynamically linking to other smart contracts, but this effectively means the smart contract developers should think carefully before deploying a contract.

Despite complications and difficulties, the notion of smart contracts is very powerful: user-defined programs can run on a neutral execution platform, the blockchain system, and cannot be altered, censored, or retrospectively tampered with. Furthermore, they can hold digital assets, like cryptocurrency or digital tokens. In effect, they enable mutually untrusting parties to transact goods of value and exchange information.

With smart contract capabilities, it becomes possible to build applications that provide their *main functionality* through smart contracts; in [19], they are referred to as Decentralized Applications (dApps). A dApp might, for instance, only have a thin UI layer, which more or less directly interacts with the smart contracts. dApps are a special class of *blockchain-based applications*, or just *blockchain applications*, i.e., applications that make significant use of blockchain. A typical blockchain application which is not a dApp might include off-chain business logic, databases, and other components—while it uses blockchain, its main functionality is not exclusively provided by smart contracts.

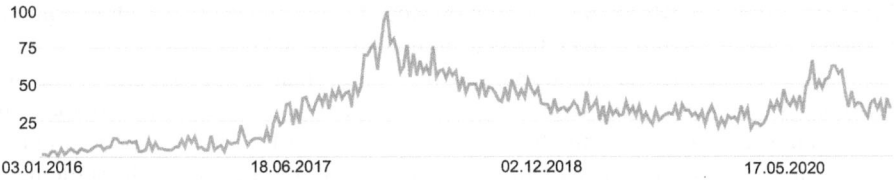

100

75

50

25

03.01.2016   18.06.2017   02.12.2018   17.05.2020

Fig. 1.2 Google Trends plot of search interest in the topic "smart contract" from 2016-01-01 to 2021-01-01; normalized relative to a peak of 100. Data source: Google Trends (https://www.google.com/trends)

1.3 Interest in Blockchain and Smart Contracts

Like many innovations, smart contract-enabled blockchain technology may be subject to Amara's law: "We tend to overestimate the effect of a technology in the short run and underestimate the effect in the long run." This law is, to a degree, expressed and refined in Gartner's *Hype Cycle*: after a promising new technology is introduced, attention rises dramatically, to so-called peak of *inflated* expectations. Because many of these expectations were inflated, at least in the short run, what follows is the "trough of disillusionment." Eventually, technologies are matched with the areas in which they add real value, which leads via the "slope of enlightenment" to the "plateau of productivity" in the hype cycle.

While the hype cycle has been scrutinized and criticized [13, 14], as a mental model it is useful and can be related to the attention blockchain and smart contracts have received. Google Trends[1] shows levels of interest in the topic "smart contract" that actually match the hype cycle relatively well, as depicted in Fig. 1.2. The peak of attention is around December 2017/January 2018, when the exchange rates for the cryptocurrencies Bitcoin and Ether surged, while the low point in search interest following the peak is roughly in 2019. Note that the above discussion is only illustrative, indicative at best. A much more detailed analysis and discussion of the status quo in 2019, with a particular view on Australia, and how the productivity plateau may be reached is subject to the report "Blockchain 2030" [2].

But why is there so much attention and interest in the topic? As Xu et al. state [19]: "blockchain applications have the potential to disrupt the fabric of society, industry, and government." In order words: the way we interact across the boundaries of organizations and individuals may be subject to innovation based on blockchain technology. It may not be the best solution for many cases, though [19], but it does offer an alternative. In fact, blockchain has been investigated in almost all industries [2]. A few example use cases, where blockchain offers an interesting alternative, are listed below.

---

[1] https://trends.google.com/, last accessed 2021-02-08.

Stock Exchange Settlements Trading on stock exchanges is often high in volume and requires low latency. Given the typical non-functional properties of blockchain applications, described also in the next section, blockchain is not a natural candidate technology for such trading engines. However, in many countries the settlement of stock trades takes days. During this time, the money for the trades is tied up in the settlement processes. Blockchain or DLT can be used for speeding up the settlement processes from days to minutes or even seconds, such that billions of dollars can be freed up. The Australian Securities Exchange (ASX) has been working on switching to a DLT-based solution for settlement since 2016.[2]

Collaborative Business Processes Integration of business processes across organizational boundaries can result in strong productivity gains. However, integrating IT systems implementing the processes has traditionally been the exclusive playing field of large companies and/or few processes with few business partners, such as in the automotive industry. Based on blockchain and DLT, smart contracts can be used to implement multi-party business processes, even when mutual trust among business partners is low. This approach has been pioneered in [15], and a broad view on the topic is presented in [8]. Chapter 3 discusses the topic and a particular system, Caterpillar, in detail.

Food Tracking and Agricultural Supply Chains Tracing food from "farm to fork" is a goal that has been pursued by many players in the food industry in recent years, in order to achieve higher food quality, higher consumer confidence in labels like "organic," and greater supply chain transparency. Since agricultural supply chains often involve many parties, and these may not know (of) each other, let alone trust one-another, blockchain is a natural candidate technology for achieving the goal. Furthermore, counterparty risks are commonly found in agricultural supply chains. Blockchain allows tokenizing agricultural assets and tracking ownership, thus lowering the trust requirement for transacting with other parties [19, Chapter 12]. Finally, the tokenized assets enable new forms of financing [12], such that, e.g., a bank can readily provide a loan against an agricultural asset.

To identify promising use cases in a given context, such as for a company or government agency, the approach in [5] can be used.

1.4 Overview of Architectural Concerns for Blockchain Applications

When designing a blockchain application, software architects need to understand the functional and non-functional properties of blockchain as an architectural element.

---

[2]https://www2.asx.com.au/markets/clearing-and-settlement-services/chess-replacement/about-chess-replacement, last accessed 2021-02-11.

As described in [19, Chapter 5], blockchain can serve the following four main roles:

- Communication mechanism: transactions that are announced to the blockchain network are communicated to all nodes, either before or after inclusion in a block;
- Data store, for data attached to transactions or stored as part of the state of smart contracts;
- Computation, through the code in smart contracts; and
- Asset control and management mechanism, in that assets can be created, transferred, traded, swapped, and destroyed, relatively safely and easily and without relying on a trusted third party. While this role is fulfilled as a combination of the previous three, asset control is a stand-out feature of blockchains and therefore listed as a separate role in the book.

However, before actually designing such an application, the *suitability* of blockchain should be assessed critically. To this end, a number of decision processes have been proposed in the literature, including [7, 11, 17] and [19, Chapter 6].

In case the suitability assessment comes to an affirmative result and blockchain should indeed be used, then the actual *design process* starts. The design process should decide, among many other aspects, which of the four roles mentioned above blockchain should play in the system being designed and for which parts of it. That is, for all four roles the decision needs to be made in terms of: what should be on-chain, and what should be off-chain? In more detail:

1. Which messages should be communicated via the blockchain and which through other channels?
2. Which data should be stored on the blockchain (on-chain) and which off-chain?
3. Which parts of the computation should be done on-chain in smart contracts, and which off-chain?
4. Are there assets that can be managed through DLT? Should they be managed in such a way?

Other relevant questions in the context of the design process include decentralization —is there a trusted authority, and if so, (how) can it be decentralized? Which blockchain or DLT should be used and how should it be configured (including block configuration)? Where and how will the blockchain system be deployed and operated, so as to not create (among others) risks of centralization on another level? More information on all of the above can again be found in [19, Chapter 6].

For making the respective decisions in an informed way, architects need to also understand the impact on *non-functional properties*. Often, this involves trade-offs, e.g., between desired levels of confidentiality and transparency. There are also numerous other impacts, e.g., in that read availability and read latency can be very favorable in a blockchain-based application, because creating redundant replicas and reading from them are comparatively easy. In contrast, writing to a blockchain system can be harder to manage, both in terms of latency and availability—the new data needs to be validated and accepted by a network of nodes which are most often not under the control of a single organization. High degrees of integrity, however, are often achieved easily in such a system. Other non-functional properties that are commonly considered include additional aspects of dependability, security, and performance, as well as cost.

1.5   Overview of Blockchain Design Patterns

With the relative recent rise of blockchain and DLT come many new problems and opportunities. For some of those, design patterns have been proposed, among others to find DLT-suitable trade-offs. Software design patterns, originally made popular with the book of the "Gang of Four" [4], provide proven solution approaches to recurring problems. While some of the design patterns from traditional software engineering are directly applicable for blockchain-based applications, others do not fit this new context. Reasons for the latter case include less strong object orientation or expressiveness of languages for smart contracts, or because it might simply be overly costly (in the literal or a figurative sense) to implement a given pattern on blockchain.

To handle some of the new challenges and opportunities, additional patterns have been proposed. These cover general sets of patterns [16, 18], foundational patterns concerning oracles [9], i.e., how data is moved onto and out of blockchain, how to split computation between on-chain and off-chain parts [3], and more specialized topics like Self-Sovereign Identity (SSI) [6] or migration between blockchains [1].

Two concrete examples of patterns, originally proposed in [18] but also described in [19, Chapter 7], are given next. The first example pattern is called "Contract Registry" and concerns updating smart contracts. Recall from the definition of smart contracts in Sect. 1.2 that contracts are immutable once deployed. As such, updates where an old version is directly replaced with a new version are, by default, not possible with in-place substitution: the old contract code cannot be changed or replaced. Logically, however, an update can be achieved by deploying a new version of a contract, and using it instead of the old version. This is made easy by using a contract registry: the registry always points to the current version of a smart contract. This is depicted in Fig. 1.3: for $Contract_1$ and $Contract_2$, there is only one version; $Contract_3$ has been replaced with $Contract_{3'}$.

The second example pattern is called "Embedded Permissions." It addresses the problem that, for many situations, anyone on a blockchain system can call any function of any deployed smart contract. Whether or not a user should be allowed to make use of a function needs to be checked by the function itself, i.e., before executing the code that realizes the core of the function, the function checks if the caller is permitted to execute it. As such, the permission check is embedded in the function. This is shown in Fig. 1.4, where one user is allowed to execute both functions, whereas the other user is only permitted to execute one function.

Since the pattern catalogs are distributed across a number of publications, and the relation between different patters from different catalogs is non-obvious, a decision

Fig. 1.3 Contract registry pattern (source: [19])

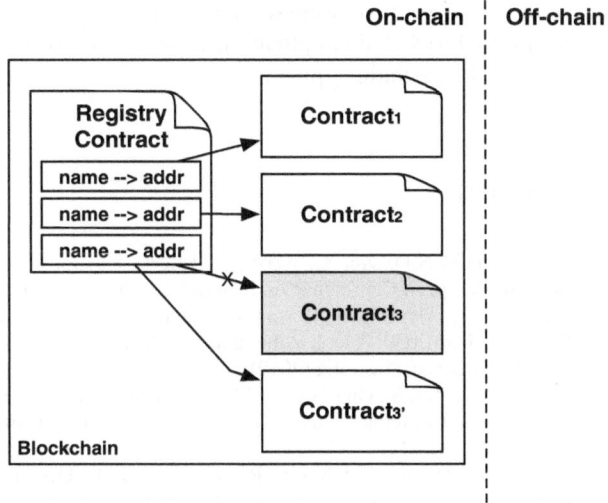

Fig. 1.4 Embedded permissions pattern (source: [19])

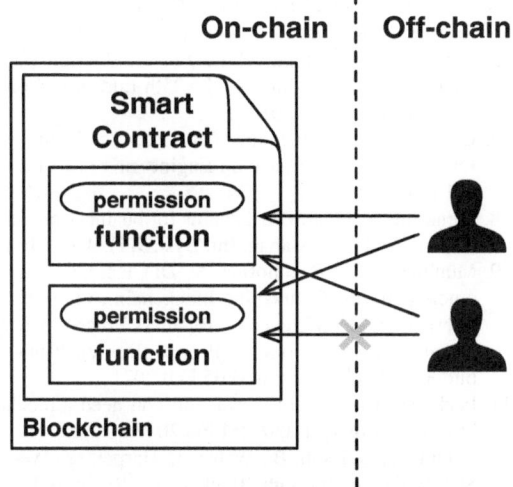

model has been proposed recently [20]. This decision model can guide architects in choosing (sets of) patterns for particular situations.

1.6 Summary

In this chapter, we gave a broad overview of blockchain and DLT, what it is and why it is used. We discussed the most important terms and introduced the concept of smart contracts. Then, we looked at the interest in the topic and discussed three use cases in brief. We also discussed the major architectural concerns, and the process of designing blockchain applications. Finally, an overview was provided on design patterns for blockchain applications.

References

1. Bandara, H.M.N.D., Xu, X., Weber, I.: Patterns for blockchain migration. In: Proceedings of the 25th European Conference on Pattern Languages of Programs (EuroPLoP '20) (2020)
2. Bratanova, A., Devaraj, D., Horton, J., Naughtin, C., Kloester, B., Trinh, K., Weber, I., Dawson, D.: Blockchain 2030: A look at the future of blockchain in Australia. Technical Report, Data61, CSIRO, Brisbane, Australia (2019)
3. Eberhardt, J., Tai, S.: On or off the blockchain? Insights on off-chaining computation and data. In: European Conference on Service-Oriented and Cloud Computing (ESOCC2017), pp. 3–15 (2017)
4. Gamma, E., Helm, R., Johnson, R., Vlissides, J.M.: Design Patterns: Elements of Reusable Object-Oriented Software, 1st edn. Addison-Wesley Professional, Boston (1994)
5. Gräther, W., Klein, S., Prinz, W.: A use case identification framework and use case canvas for identifying and exploring relevant blockchain opportunities. In: ERCIM-Blockchain 2018: Blockchain Engineering: Challenges and Opportunities for Computer Science Research, Reports of the European Society for Socially Embedded Technologies, vol. 2 (2018)
6. Liu, Y., Lu, Q., Paik, H.Y., Xu, X.: Design patterns for blockchain-based self-sovereign identity. In: Proceedings of the 25th European Conference on Pattern Languages of Programs (EuroPLoP '20) (2020)
7. Lo, S.K., Xu, X., Chiam, Y.K., Lu, Q.: Evaluating suitability of applying blockchain. In: International Conference on Engineering of Complex Computer Systems (ICECCS), pp. 158–161 (2017)
8. Mendling, J., et. al: Blockchains for business process management - challenges and opportunities. ACM Trans. Manag. Inf. Syst. **9**(1), 4:1–4:16 (2018). https://doi.org/10.1145/3183367
9. Mühlberger, R., Bachhofner, S., Di Ciccio, C., Weber, I., Wöhrer, M., Zdun, U.: Foundational oracle patterns: Connecting blockchain to the off-chain world. In: Blockchain Forum of the International Conference on Business Process Management (BPM) (2020)
10. Nakamoto, S.: Bitcoin: A Peer-to-Peer electronic cash system (2008). https://bitcoin.org/bitcoin.pdf. Last Accessed 05 Feb 2021
11. Peck, M.: Blockchain world - do you need a blockchain? IEEE Spectrum **54**, 38–60 (2017). https://doi.org/10.1109/MSPEC.2017.8048838
12. Pufahl, L., Ohlsson, B., Weber, I., Harper, G., Weston, E.: Enabling Financing in Agricultural Supply Chains through Blockchain. Business Process Management Cases, vol. 2. Springer, Berlin (2021)
13. Steinert, M., Leifer, L.: Scrutinizing Gartner's hype cycle approach. In: Technology Management for Global Economic Growth (PICMET'10), pp. 1–13 (2010)
14. Voiovich, J.T.: Unhyping the hype cycle: Five secrets to building an attention dashboard for any innovation (2019). https://medium.com/swlh/unhyping-the-hype-cycle-five-secrets-to-building-an-attention-dashboard-for-any-innovation-858a3251cd1b. Last Accessed 08 Feb 2021
15. Weber, I., Xu, X., Riveret, R., Governatori, G., Ponomarev, A., Mendling, J.: Untrusted business process monitoring and execution using blockchain. In: Proceedings of the Business Process Management - 14th International Conference, BPM 2016, Rio de Janeiro, Brazil, September 18–22, 2016, pp. 329–347 (2016). https://doi.org/10.1007/978-3-319-45348-4_19
16. Wöhrer, M., Zdun, U.: Design patterns for smart contracts in the Ethereum ecosystem. In: Proceedings of the IEEE iThings/GreenCom/CPSCom/SmartData, pp. 1513–1520 (2018)

17. Wüst, K., Gervais, A.: Do you need a blockchain? In: 2018 Crypto Valley Conference on Blockchain Technology (CVCBT), pp. 45–54 (2018)
18. Xu, X., Pautasso, C., Zhu, L., Lu, Q., Weber, I.: A pattern collection for blockchain-based applications. In: Proceedings of the 23rd European Conference on Pattern Languages of Programs (EuroPLoP '18), pp. 1–20 (2018)
19. Xu, X., Weber, I., Staples, M.: Architecture for Blockchain Applications. Springer, Berlin (2019). https://doi.org/10.1007/978-3-030-03035-3
20. Xu, X., Bandara, H.D., Lu, Q., Weber, I., Bass, L., Zhu, L.: A decision model for choosing patterns in blockchain-based applications. In: ICSA'21: IEEE International Conference on Software Architecture (2021)

Chapter 2
Extraction of Meaningful Events for Process Mining from Blockchain

Agnes Koschmider and Frank Duchmann

Abstract Smart contracts running on top of a blockchain are self-executing contracts allowing to verify the fulfillment of rules. Direct extraction of events from smart contracts for process mining is only of limited utility due to the transactional structure of blockchain records. The deployment of smart contracts on the blockchain network, however, leaves traces in terms of transactions, which can be processed in such a way as to suit process mining algorithms. This paper suggests an application layer comprised of queries allowing for the extraction of meaningful events for process mining from a blockchain. The use of process mining with smart contract executions allows us to analyze their logical flow and to identify (non)conformity. Our implementation enables the discovery of process models from smart contract executions with low latency and thus (non)conformity in smart contracts can be diagnosed efficiently by means of common quality measures.

2.1 Introduction

The blockchain is based on a decentralized peer-to-peer network, which makes use of cryptography to securely host applications and store data, "where non-trusting members can interact with each other without a trusted intermediary in a verifiable manner" [4]. Smart contracts running on top of a blockchain are self-executing contracts allowing to verify the fulfillment of rules. The execution of a smart contract precedes the coding of the contract in a programming language (e.g., Solidity). When all predefined conditions are met, smart contracts are put into effect. The deployment of smart contracts on a blockchain network leaves traces in terms of transactions, which could be exploited by process mining. Process mining has

A. Koschmider (✉)
Group Process Analytics, Kiel University, Kiel, Germany
e-mail: ak@informatik.uni-kiel.de

F. Duchmann
EnBW Energie Baden-Württemberg AG, Karlsruhe, Germany

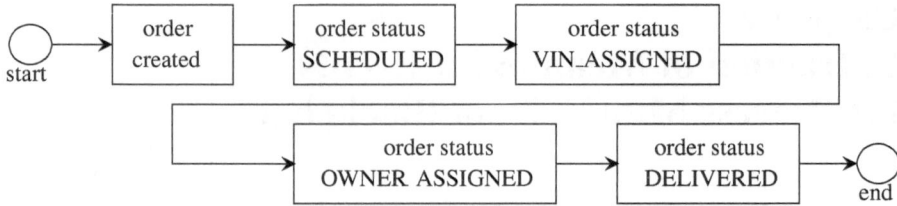

Fig. 2.1 Process of the vehicle manufacturing network smart contract that is used for illustration purposes throughout the paper

demonstrated many benefits for various domains, such as unveiling hidden tasks or patterns [12]. Process mining takes event logs, records the sequence of steps, and discovers the model of a corresponding process. Mandatory attributes of an event log are a case ID, activity, and timestamp. Although transactions of a blockchain are logged, the logs cannot directly be mapped onto an event log for process mining since they do not fulfill the mandatory structure of event logs. Instead, blockchain records have a transactional data structure. To bridge the gap, this paper suggests an application layer comprising of two queries allowing to extract meaningful events for process mining from a blockchain. We motivate the use of process mining techniques for a blockchain by the example shown in Fig. 2.1. This figure visualizes the process of the freely available vehicle manufacturing network smart contract.[1] This smart contract tracks manufacturing data of vehicles from an initial order request (i.e., order creation) to the delivery by the manufacturer. The properties of this smart contract are shown in Fig. 2.2, see input of the activity "include contract into blockchain." The contract has the properties "Participants: Person, Regulator, Manufacturer," "Assets: Order, Vehicle," and "Transactions: PlaceOrder, Update-OrderStatus, SetupDemo." The transaction "PlaceOrder," for instance, creates a new order with details about the customer. With the "UpdateOrderStatus" transaction, the manufacturer transmits the current status of the order; e.g., "OrderStatus" can be changed from PLACED to "SCHEDULED_FOR_MANUFACTURE." Once the vehicle has been manufactured, the producer registers the vehicle with the transaction "UpdateOrderStatus" and the status is changed to "VIN_ASSIGNED." Subsequently, the vehicle owner is assigned by the field "OWNER_ASSIGNED." After vehicle delivery, the status is set to "DELIVERED" in the "updateOrder-Status" transaction. The smart contract becomes part of a blockchain after it has been deployed to a blockchain network. Subsequently, process mining in terms of conformance checking allows to identify (non)conformance issues by querying the blockchain. In this way, our approach allows to diagnose (non)conformity in smart contracts by means of common process mining quality measures.

---

[1] https://www.npmjs.com/package/vehicle-manufacture-network.

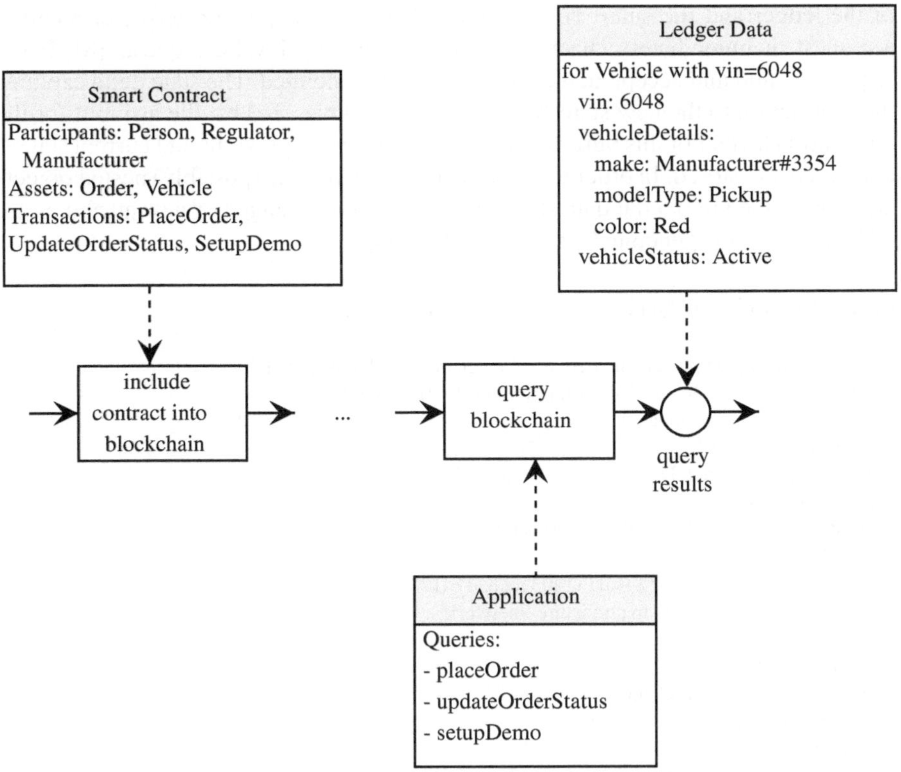

Smart Contract
Participants: Person, Regulator, Manufacturer
Assets: Order, Vehicle
Transactions: PlaceOrder, UpdateOrderStatus, SetupDemo

Ledger Data

for Vehicle with vin=6048
  vin: 6048
  vehicleDetails:
    make: Manufacturer#3354
    modelType: Pickup
    color: Red
  vehicleStatus: Active

include contract into blockchain

...

query blockchain

query results

Application
Queries: - placeOrder - updateOrderStatus - setupDemo

Fig. 2.2 The smart contract becomes part of the blockchain after it has been deployed to a blockchain network

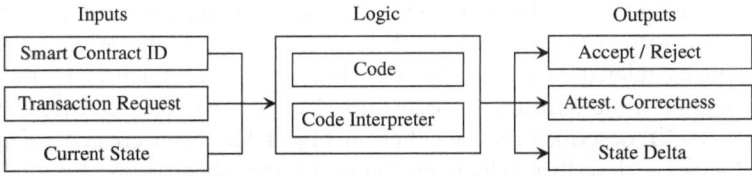

Inputs	Logic	Outputs
Smart Contract ID	Code	Accept / Reject
Transaction Request	Code Interpreter	Attest. Correctness
Current State		State Delta

Fig. 2.3 This figure shows how smart contracts process requests, see [8]

2.2 Application Layer to Extract Events for Process Mining

The intention of our application layer is to extract meaningful events from smart contracts in order to make them accessible to process mining. For this purpose, changes in terms of newly added records to the distributed ledger (i.e., the blockchain) are compared. Figure 2.3 shows how smart contracts process requests. Smart contract inputs include the contract identifier, the transaction request, and the current state of the ledger. The code interpreter is loaded with the current state

of the ledger and the smart contract code. When the contract interpreter receives
a request, it immediately checks and then rejects any invalid requests [8]. If the
request is valid and accepted, then a state delta is generated. The state delta captures
the transaction to the new state. We regard the `state delta` file as input for the
application layer. For this purpose, the delta between the previous and current state is
compared and stored. In order to identify state changes, the (possibly) nested objects
are transformed into a flat data structure. If a value is changed or new attributes are
added, an event is generated, as explained below.

Listing 2.1 A meaningful event extracted from a blockchain

```
1   {
2     key: "Asset:org.acme.vehicle_network.Vehicle0812e6d8d486e0464",
3     timestamp: "Mon Dec 31 2018 14:47:01 GMT+0100 (CET)",
4     eventLevel1: "asset updated",
5     eventLevel1Id: "2",
6     eventLevel2: "vehicleDetails.colour changed",
7     eventLevel2Id: "3",
8     eventLevel3: "vehicleDetails.colour:Red > Blue",
9     eventLevel3Id: "15",
10    tx_id: "44f1e85ca5fba82d04df1114031ee8247d17393a9c79c413",
11    chaincode_id: "vehicle−manufacture−network",
12    block_number: "5",
13    endorser: "Org1MSP",
14    channelId: "composerchannel",
15    creatorMSP: "Org1MSP",
16    registryType: "Asset",
17    assetClass: "org.acme.vehicle_network.Vehicle"
18  },
```

An event is defined by an ID (key), a timestamp, attributes referring to the level of
events called `eventLevel` and blockchain-specific attributes (see Listing 2.1).
The attributes related to `eventLevel` describe the abstraction of the object
status ranging from abstract (`eventLevel1`) to concrete (`eventLevel3`).
`eventLevel1` describes the fact that an object has been created or updated.
`eventLevel2` describes which attributes of the object have been changed.
`eventLevel3` describes the concrete change of the object. Table 2.1 shows
examples of these levels. To determine the level of events, we further distinguish
between simple and complex events and, to this end, introduce the function
`eventDefinition`.

Table 2.1 Different event levels are attached to an event specifying what object and how it has
been changed

	Create	Update
eventLevel1	Asset created	Asset updated
eventLevel2	Vehicle created	Color.color changed
eventLevel3	Vehicle created with id=123	Color.color changed from blue to red

Simple Event A simple event is defined at runtime and describes the difference between the current state and the state delta. Generally, process mining could be employed for simple events. However, for a large data set, as is the case for blockchains, this would result in spaghetti-like process models with many irrelevant events. To enable the discovery of block-structured process models, we define the notion of complex events.

Complex Event Complex events aggregate or filter simple events. To define complex events based on simple events, we use the following syntax:

- a term is a unit opened with [and closed with].
- terms can be combined through a logical AND (represented by **&&**) or a logical OR (represented by ||).
- terms can be structured by parenthesis (,).
- a term is structured in the following way: *attribute = regular expression referring to the input state > regular expression referring to the current state*.

Table 2.2 shows the application of the formal syntax using the example of the vehicle manufacturing smart contract from Fig. 2.2.

To determine the `eventDefinition` attribute, we evaluate regular expressions. Table 2.3 shows some evaluations of regular expressions. If both expressions are evaluated as true, the resulting value is true as well and an event is logged in the event log. If one of the regular expressions is false, the result is false and no event is generated.

Table 2.2 Definition of complex events with regular expressions

eventLevel	eventName	eventDefinition
eventLevel1	Owner changed	[owner = .* > .*]
eventLevel3	Andy has a car	[owner = .* > Person.Andy]
eventLevel2	Skylights ordered	[vehicleDetails.1 = no > yes]
eventLevel2	Transfer to Person	[owner = Company.* > Person.*]
eventLevel3	Color type changed metallic to matt	[color.type = metallic > matt]
eventLevel2	Value and owner changed	[owner = .* > .*] && [value = .* > .*]

Table 2.3 Evaluation of regular expressions

Typ	Event evaluation
Definition	[color.color = .* > red]
RegEx	oldStruct['color.color'].regexp('.*') && newStruct['color.color'].regexp('red')
Evaluation	True && true
Return value	True

2.3   Implementation

We implemented the extraction of events from a blockchain for Hyperledger Fabric, Hyperledger Composer, and IBM Blockchain Platform, which differ in their authentication processes. Although we also included Ethereum initially, we stopped working with this platform for several reasons. Ethereum does not primarily target business-related smart contracts and thus the use of our approach is only of little relevance. Furthermore, when we applied our approach to Ethereum we discovered that too many empty blocks were mined, which unnecessarily expands and complicates the event log. Therefore, we decided to continue with Hyperledger Fabric, Hyperledger Composer, and IBM Blockchain Platform and plan to work with Ethereum in the future.

Our approach employs two queries queryChain and getProcessLog within the following three steps:

1. Connection to Hyperledger Fabric network and download of blockchain.
2. Event extraction.
3. Event log export.

Step 1:   Connection to Hyperledger Fabric network and download of blockchain: The query queryChain requests to register on the blockchain and returns ledger blocks as JSON objects. Communication with Hyperledger Fabric instances is implemented with NodeJS SDK.

Step 2:   Event extraction: A direct extraction of events from the smart contract is not useful since the transactional structure returns too many irrelevant events. Instead, as explained above, complex events are aggregated or filtered from simple events. This process of event extraction is shown in Fig. 2.4. This step of our approach is implemented with the getProcessLog query, which extracts events from block writes in the blockchain. Block writes are the parts of a block that contain lists of unique IDs and the associated key value pairs that are written by a transaction.

Each block consists of the mandatory fields header, data, and meta. The header stores data related to the block number, the hash value of the previous block, and the hash value of its own block. Meta stores the signature of the membership service provider and the ordering person. While header and meta do not refer to any user data, the data fields refer to all executed transactions. Each transaction is further refined in the fields header, signature, proposal, response, and endorsements. The response field contains user data including the write field, which describes the state change of the ledger with key value pairs. The block write contains a list of unique keys (though there can be an overlap with the keys present in the read set) and their new values as written by the transaction. If the update implemented by the transaction is to delete the key, a delete marker is set for the key instead of a new value. Further, if the transaction writes multiple

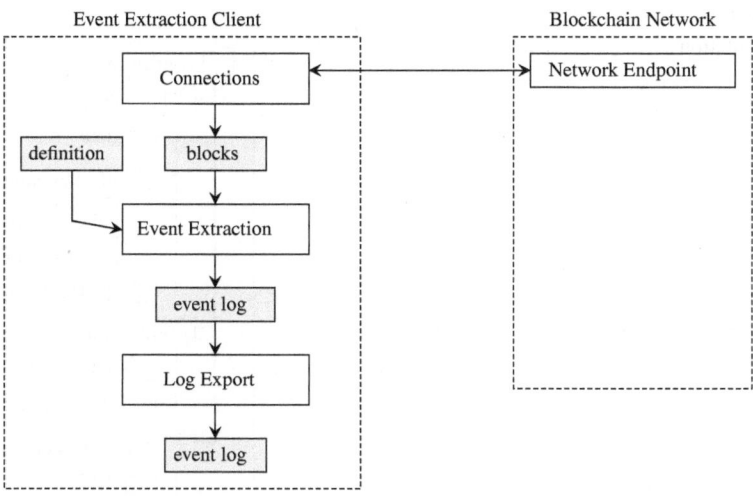

Fig. 2.4 Architecture of event extraction

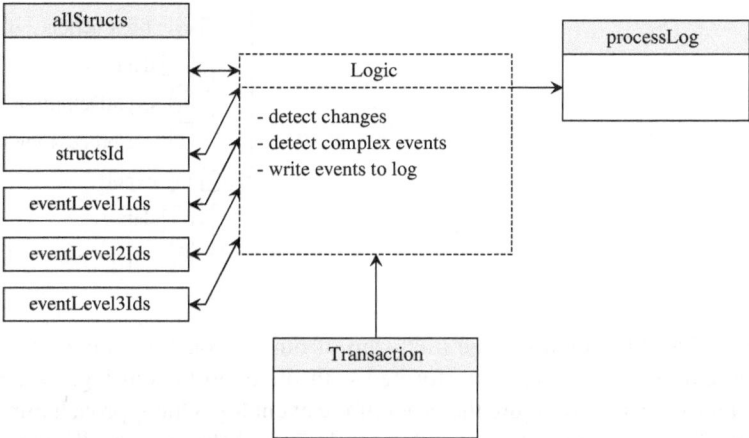

Fig. 2.5 Data structure of the get-event-log script

values for a key, we only continue with the last written value. See Fig. 2.6 for the data structure of the get-event-log script. The results of the event log extraction are stored in a JSON file called event extraction/data, and this file is then used as input for step 3 of our approach (Fig. 2.5).

Figure 2.6 shows the file structure of the implementation.

Fig. 2.6 File structure of the implementation

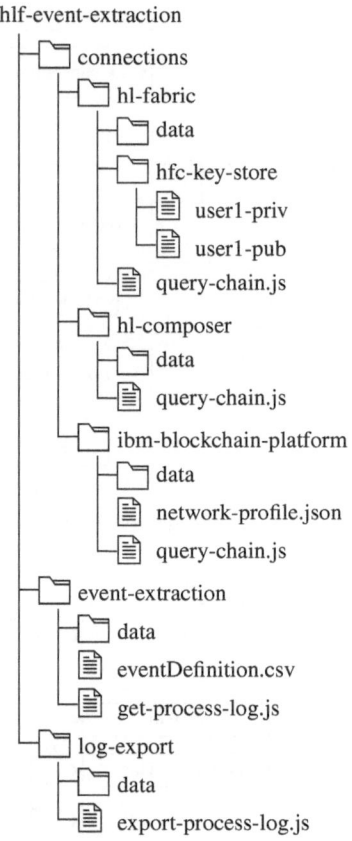

Step 3:   Event log export. The final step of our approach is to export the event log in csv format, which is performed with the export-event-log.js script. This script allows us to configure the order of the event log. Our approach implements a multi-level sort order. The event log can be sorted chronologically according to the time sequence of events, according to the case ID and the date format. The date file can be configured according to the format YYYY.HH.mm.ss or YYYY-MM-DD'T'HH:mm:ss.

Table 2.4 shows the event log for the vehicle manufacture network smart contracts. The implementation of our approach allows us to generate a process model with limited latency following the smart contract execution. The source code of our project can be downloaded from https://github.com/FrankDuchmann/hf-event-extraction.

Table 2.4 Event log exported from the csv file

CaseID	timestamp	eventLevel2	eventLevel3
Order#o1	08.05.2019 11.32.36	Order created	Asset—Order created
Order#o1	08.05.2019 11.32.46	OrderStatus changed	OrderStatus:SCHEDULED_FOR_MA...
Order#o1	08.05.2019 11.32.56	OrderStatus changed	OrderStatus:VIN_ASSIGNED
Order#o1	08.05.2019 11.33.06	OrderStatus changed	OrderStatus:OWNER_ASSIGNED
Order#o1	08.05.2019 11.33.16	OrderStatus changed	OrderStatus:DELIVERED
Order#o2	08.05.2019 11.32.36	Order created	asset—Order created
Order#o2	08.05.2019 11.32.56	OrderStatus changed	OrderStatus:VIN_ASSIGNED
Order#o2	08.05.2019 11.33.06	OrderStatus changed	OrderStatus:OWNER_ASSIGNED
Order#o2	08.05.2019 11.33.16	OrderStatus changed	OrderStatus:DELIVERED
Order#o3	08.05.2019 11.32.36	Order created	Asset—Order created
Order#o3	08.05.2019 11.32.46	OrderStatus changed	OrderStatus:SCHEDULED_FOR_MA...
Order#o3	08.05.2019 11.32.56	OrderStatus changed	OrderStatus:VIN_ASSIGNED
Order#o3	08.05.2019 11.33.06	OrderStatus changed	OrderStatus:OWNER_ASSIGNED
Order#o3	08.05.2019 11.33.16	OrderStatus changed	OrderStatus:DELIVERED
Order#o4	08.05.2019 11.32.36	Order created	asset—Order created
Order#o4	08.05.2019 11.32.56	OrderStatus changed	OrderStatus:VIN_ASSIGNED

2.4 Application

In this section, we demonstrate the feasibility of our approach using the vehicle manufacturing network smart contract from Hyperledger Composer.

2.4.1 Preparation

First, a running instance of Hyperledger Composer and the deployed vehicle manufacturing network smart contract are required. Next, the scripts setupDemo and generateDemoData must be executed. In addition, some transactions of the updateOrderStatus function must be called. This creates 11 instances of the process vehicle manufacturing network smart contract (see Fig. 2.2). After all dependencies are installed, the script connections/hl-com-poser/queryChain.js is executed. This establishes a connection, downloads the individual blocks of the blockchain, and saves them as a JSON file. Next, the events are extracted using the getProcessLog.js script. If the execution is completed, the temporary event log is located under /event-extraction/data/ and then the event log export takes place. In the configuration of the /log-export/export-csv.js script, the user can set the parameters for sorting events. Furthermore, the input file and the name of the output file must be set. After executing this script, a csv file is created under /log-export/data/vmn log.csv. This event log can then be used for process mining as described in the next section. Fig. 2.7 shows the output of the getProcessLog.js script.

2.4.2 Process Discovery and Conformance Checking

We applied two process mining algorithms (i.e., alpha algorithm and the heuristic miner) to the event log of the vehicle manufacturing network example. Figure 2.8 shows the discovered process model with the heuristic miner using a threshold of 0.1. We also used the Disco tool[2] to discover a process model from an event log (see Fig. 2.9). The color intensity of the nodes and the thickness of arcs describe the frequency with which activities occur in the event log.

Finally, we applied conformance checking (i.e., token replay) to the vehicle manufacturing networks example, which requires a process model and an event log as inputs. For this, we used the event log from Table 2.4 and the process model from Fig. 2.10. Figure 2.11 shows the result. The analysis of the process models indicates that two process instances skip the activity "OWNER_ASSIGNED" and directly execute the activity "order status DELIVERED." In addition, the analysis shows that the process has not been completed yet since not every manufactured car has been assigned to an owner.

2.5   Related Work

The use of blockchain technologies in Business Process Management (BPM) has been thoroughly discussed in previous scholarship, including the possibility of mining processes based on blockchain transaction data [10]. Related works addressing smart contract analysis can be distinguished by the time point of the analysis. Approaches related to compile time aim to identify syntax or type checking errors (see [1] for further reference). Runtime-based analyses try to identify semantic errors [2, 3, 7]. In contrast to these existing approaches to verification of smart contracts based on semantic errors [2, 3, 7], this paper suggests a process mining approach and goes beyond existing work in the following ways. Our approach does not require that additional smart contract properties are specified as is the case in [2, 7]. Instead, in our approach, the logical flow of smart contracts is analyzed in terms of conformance checking, which indicates areas for improvement.

To the best of our knowledge, the number of process mining approaches using data from blockchains is very small. Related approaches use smart contracts as cleaning of event logs [6] or suggest a distributed architecture allowing parallel processing of event log data to generate a XES file [9]. We have ourselves

---

[2]https://fluxicon.com/disco/.

```
Check Object with id=Asset:org.acme.vehicle_network.Order02          getProcessLog.js:408
Property orderStatus changed from VIN_ASSIGNED to OWNER_ASSIGNED     getProcessLog.js:246
detect complex events ...                                           getProcessLog.js:260
  Definition1                                                       getProcessLog.js:105
  owner assigned: false                                             getProcessLog.js:108
  Definition2                                                       getProcessLog.js:132
  vin assigned to car: false                                        getProcessLog.js:108
  Definition3                                                       getProcessLog.js:132
  vehicleStatus changed to ACTIVE: false                            getProcessLog.js:147
detect complex events ... [done]                                    getProcessLog.js:339
Event1 asset updated                                                getProcessLog.js:340
Event2 orderStatus changed                                          getProcessLog.js:341
Event3 orderStatus:VIN_ASSIGNED > OWNER_ASSIGNED                    getProcessLog.js:246
Check Object with id=Asset:org.acme.vehicle_network.Vehicle:vin_2   getProcessLog.js:260
Property vehicleStatus changed from OFF_THE_ROAD to ACTIVE          getProcessLog.js:260
Property owner changed from undefined to Person#Hanna               getProcessLog.js:105
detect complex events ...                                           getProcessLog.js:108
  Definition1                                                       getProcessLog.js:132
  owner assigned: true                                              getProcessLog.js:143
  emmit complex event: owner assigned                               getProcessLog.js:108
  Definition2                                                       getProcessLog.js:132
  vin assigned to car: false                                        getProcessLog.js:108
  Definition3                                                       getProcessLog.js:143
  vehicleStatus changed to ACTIVE: true                             getProcessLog.js:147
  emmit complex event: vehicleStatus changed to ACTIVE             getProcessLog.js:405
detect complex events ... [done]                                    getProcessLog.js:406
Inspecting Block 11 [done]                                           getProcessLog.js:407
                                                                    getProcessLog.js:408
------------------------------                                      getProcessLog.js:191
| Block 12                    |                                     getProcessLog.js:192
Inspecting Block 12 [...]                                           getProcessLog.js:193
Check Object with id=Asset:org.acme.vehicle_network.Order04         getProcessLog.js:260
Property orderStatus changed from OWNER_ASSIGNED to DELIVERED        getProcessLog.js:246
detect complex events ...                                           getProcessLog.js:105
  Definition1                                                       getProcessLog.js:108
  owner assigned: false                                             getProcessLog.js:132
  Definition2                                                       getProcessLog.js:108
```

Fig. 2.7 Example output of the getProcessLog.js script

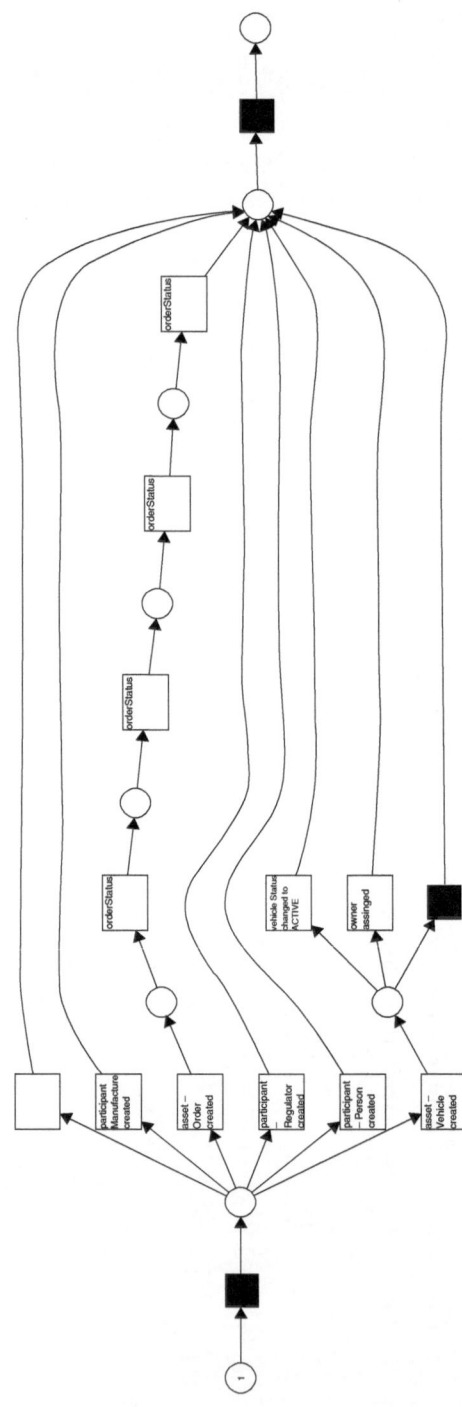

Fig. 2.8 Discovered process model from the vehicle manufacturing network smart contract using the heuristic miner

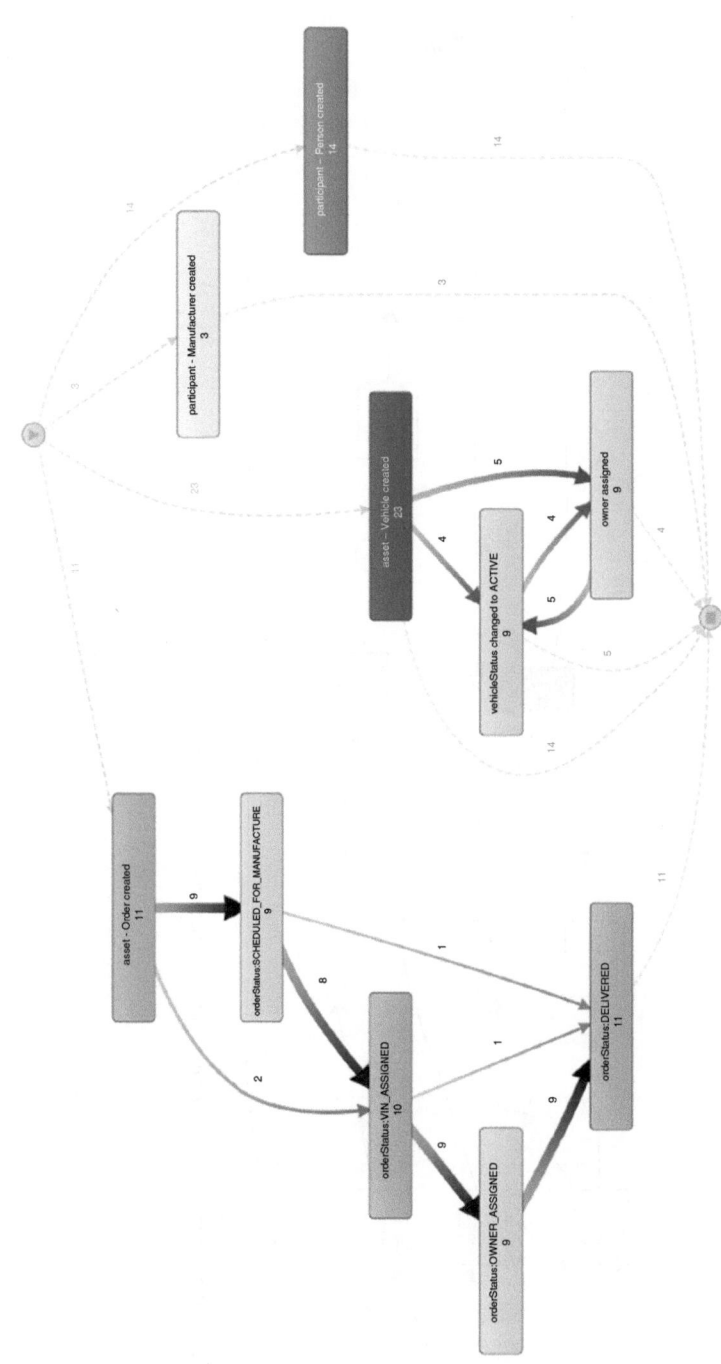

Fig. 2.9 Process model generated from a smart contract

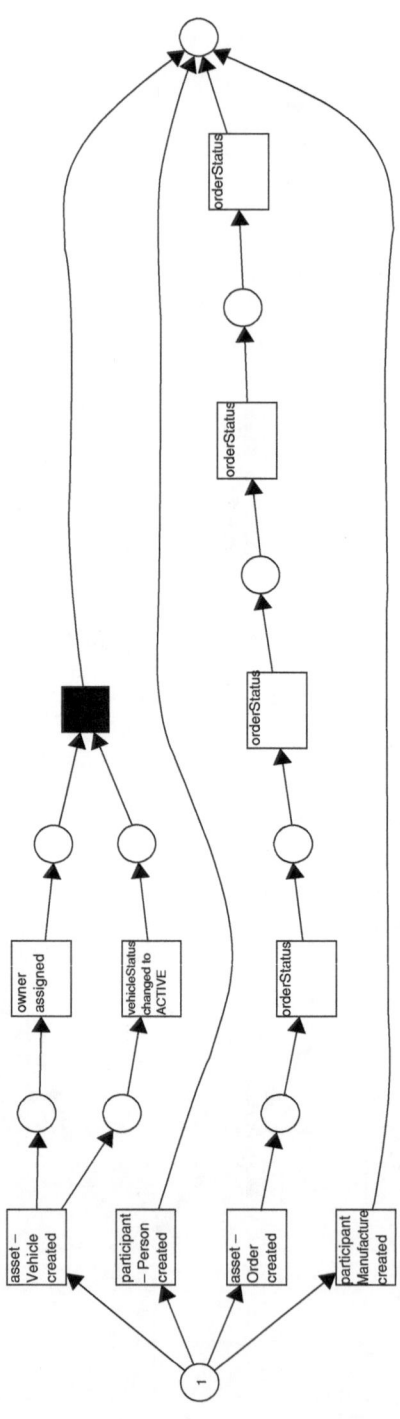

Fig. 2.10 Process model of the *vehicle manufacturing network* smart contracts

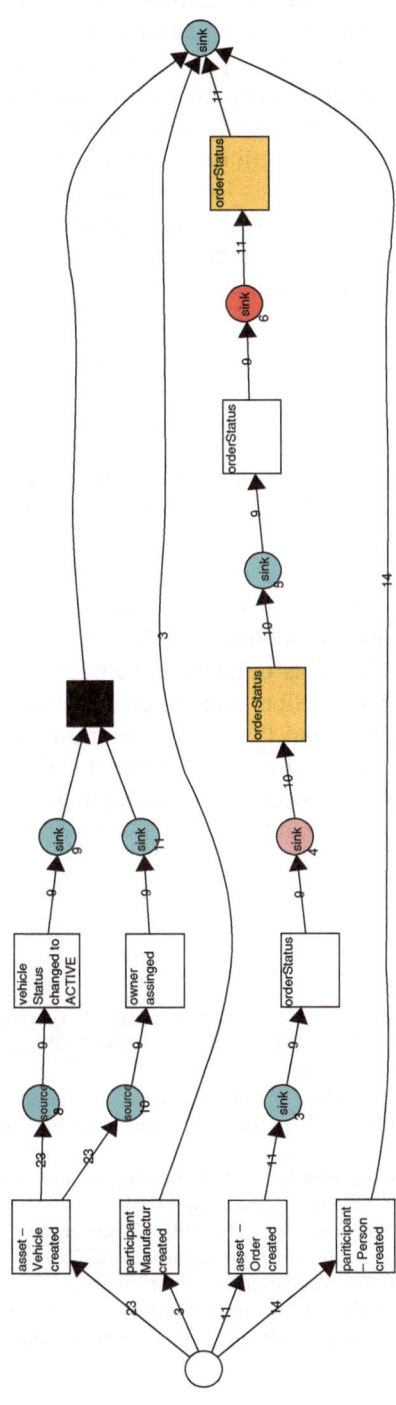

Fig. 2.11 Result of token replay

summarized the general idea of event extraction from blockchains elsewhere [5], but without describing the implementation and presenting the application of our approach. One other example of heuristic process mining is provided by Müller and Ruppel for the Ethereum blockchain [11]. In contrast to our work, the authors only allow for the use of one process mining algorithm, while our approach is open for arbitrary process mining algorithms. Müller and Ruppel also focus on extracting a number of common transaction types from blockchains, while it is our goal to identify complex events on the level of business processes. Notably, the authors give no information regarding the data extraction format they use. Nevertheless, this approach comes closest to the work at hand.

2.6 Conclusion

This paper presents an approach for event log extraction from Hyperledger Fabric and Composer. Although transactions of a blockchain are logged, the logs themselves are of little use for process mining due to their transactional data structure, which cannot be directly mapped to an event log. To bridge this gap, we implement an approach for event log extraction from a blockchain, producing event logs that can be used by any process mining tool. The use of process mining with smart contract executions allows us to analyze their logical flow and to identify (non)conformity. Our implementation enables the discovery of process models from smart contract executions and thus (non)conformity in smart contracts can be diagnosed efficiently by means of common quality measures.

Because this approach was not successful when applied to Ethereum, in the future we plan to provide a solution for event log extraction from that platform as well.

References

1. Amani, S., Bégel, M., Bortin, M., Staples, M.: Towards verifying ethereum smart contract bytecode in Isabelle/HOL. In: Proceedings of the 7th ACM SIGPLAN, CPP 2018, pp. 66–77. ACM, New York (2018)
2. Azzopardi, S., Ellul, J., Pace, G.J.: Monitoring smart contracts: Contractlarva and open challenges beyond. In: Colombo, C., Leucker, M. (eds.) Runtime Verification, pp. 113–137. Springer, Berlin (2018)
3. Azzopardi, S., Pace, G.J., Schapachnik, F.: On Observing Contracts: Deontic Contracts Meet Smart Contracts, pp. 21–30. IOS Press, Amsterdam (2018)
4. Dannen, C.: Introducing Ethereum and Solidity: Foundations of Cryptocurrency and Blockchain Programming for Beginners. Apress, New York (2017)
5. Duchmann, F., Koschmider, A.: Validation of smart contracts using process mining (short paper). In: Proceedings of the 11th Central European Workshop on Services and their Composition, Bayreuth, Germany, 2019, pp. 13–16 (2019).   http://ceur-ws.org/Vol-2339/paper3.pdf

6. Ekici, B., Tarhan, A., Ozsoy, A.: Data cleaning for process mining with smart contract. In: 2019 4th International Conference on Computer Science and Engineering (UBMK), pp. 1–6 (2019). https://doi.org/10.1109/UBMK.2019.8907140
7. Ellul, J., Pace, G.J.: Runtime verification of ethereum smart contracts. In: 2018 14th European Dependable Computing Conference (EDCC), pp. 158–163. IEEE Computer Society, Washington (2018)
8. Hyperledger Architecture: Volume ii. Technical Report. https://www.hyperledger.org
9. Klinkmüller, C., Ponomarev, A., Tran, A.B., Weber, I., van der Aalst, W.M.P.: Mining blockchain processes: Extracting process mining data from blockchain applications. In: Ciccio, C.D., Gabryelczyk, R., García-Bañuelos, L., Hernaus, T., Hull, R., Stemberger, M.I., Ko, A., Staples, M. (eds.) Proceedings of the Business Process Management: Blockchain and Central and Eastern Europe Forum - BPM 2019 Blockchain and CEE Forum, Vienna, September 1–6, 2019. Lecture Notes in Business Information Processing, vol. 361, pp. 71–86. Springer, Berlin (2019). https://doi.org/10.1007/978-3-030-30429-4_6
10. Mendling, J., Weber, I., van der Aalst, W., Cabanillas, C., Daniel, F., Debois, S., Ciccio, C.D., Dumas, M., Dustdar, S., Gal, A., Garcia-Banuelos, L., Governatori, G., Hull, R., Rosa, M.L., Leopold, H., Leymann, F., Recker, J., Reichert, M., Reijers, H.A., Rinderle-Ma, S., Rogge-Solti, A., Rosemann, M., Schulte, S., Singh, M.P., Slaats, T., Staples, M., Weber, B., Weidlich, M., Weske, M., Xu, X., Zhu, L.: Blockchains for business process management – challenges and opportunities. ACM Trans. Manag. Inf. Syst. 9(1) (2018). https://doi.org/10.1145/3183367
11. Müller, M., Ruppel, P.: Process mining for decentralized applications. In: 2019 IEEE International Conference on Decentralized Applications and Infrastructures (DAPPCON), pp. 164–169 (2019). https://doi.org/10.1109/DAPPCON.2019.00031
12. van der Aalst, W.M.P.: Process Mining - Data Science in Action, 2nd edn. Springer, Berlin (2016)

Chapter 3
Challenges of Blockchain-Based Collaborative Business Processes: An Overview of the Caterpillar System

Orlenys López Pintado

Abstract Nowadays, organizations need to manage collaborative business processes that span beyond their organizational boundaries to provide better services to their customers. However, the lack of trust among the participants is still a roadblock to implementing this type of process. In this setting, Caterpillar emerged among the prototypes to automate the execution of collaborative processes on top of the blockchain taking advantage of this technology's trust-enhancing capabilities and offering the development convenience of traditional Business Process Management Systems (BPMSs). This chapter discusses some fundamental principles and challenges to execute blockchain-based collaborative business processes. Among those, it analyzes why Caterpillar promotes single-pool processes instead of choreographies on blockchain-based processes. It also describes the advantages and trade-offs of compiled and interpreted approaches to implement processes as smart contracts. The chapter also provides an overview of the Caterpillar system functioning and concludes by outlining some challenges and open research directions.

3.1 Introduction

Business processes are a core asset of organizations. They integrate systems, data, and resources to accomplish organizational goals by delivering a service or product to a client [2]. While traditional intra-organizational processes focus on one organization, collaborative inter-organizational processes, on the other hand, span multiple organizations. Nowadays, increasing pressures on organizations to comply with globalization's growing demands have heightened the importance of collaborative processes. However, the lack of trust among organizations is a significant roadblock to implementing and executing collaborative processes, which traditionally leads to companies relying on trusted third parties to serve as mediators [9].

O. L. Pintado (✉)
Institute of Computer Science, University of Tartu, Tartu, Estonia

© The Author(s), under exclusive license to Springer Nature Switzerland AG 2021　　　31
A. Koschmider, S. Schulte (eds.), *Blockchain and Robotic Process Automation*,
https://doi.org/10.1007/978-3-030-81409-0_3

In the past decade, blockchain technology has emerged as a generic solution to enable a set of parties to collaborate in the absence of mutual trust. Blockchain technology allows a group of parties to maintain an immutable, distributed ledger of transactions and to deploy computer programs called smart contracts, allowing executing business rules as blockchain transactions. These features offer a core for running collaborative business processes between mutually untrusted parties. However, the need for highly specialized teams, which are difficult to put together, still hampers blockchain's adoption to execute business processes.[1] In contrast, Business Process Management Systems (BPMSs) provide a suitable platform to develop process-oriented applications on the blockchain[7, 9]. For example, a BPMS can automate the process execution so that process participants interact with high-level and graphical models. Simultaneously, the system can handle the low-level interactions with the blockchain, e.g., transforming models into smart contracts, generating, deploying, recovering transactions from the blockchain, etc.

This chapter explores the Caterpillar system: a prototype of BPMS to automate the execution of collaborative business processes, written in the Business Process Model and Notation (BPMN) [11], emphasizing on exploiting the blockchain capabilities to provide a tamper-proof implementation under the dynamic scenarios existing in collaborative processes. The remainder of the chapter is structured as follows. Section 3.2 introduces concepts and properties of the blockchain technology. Next, Sect. 3.3 discusses some fundamental challenges and principles behind the Caterpillar system. Specifically, why to use single-pool processes instead of choreographies in the blockchain setting (Sect. 3.3.1), and the advantages and trade-offs of compiled and interpreted approaches to implement collaborative processes (Sect. 3.3.2). Then, Sect. 3.4 offers an overview of the Caterpillar system's function, and finally, Sect. 3.5 outlines open challenges.

3.2   Blockchain Technology

A blockchain is an immutable append-only ledger replicated across a network of untrusted peer nodes. The ledger is a sequence of blocks that contain an ordered set of transactions. Each block is chained to the previous one by a hash value built from the block's content. Thus, the only way to alter/delete a transaction is by reconstructing the entire chain. Some nodes, called miners, are responsible for validating and grouping transactions submitted by the users into blocks appended to the blockchain. To be accepted, a transaction must be adequately formed and signed by its creator. Besides, the miners must reach consensus in a distributed manner [15].

Existing blockchains are typically included in one of the following three categories. (1) Public blockchain networks allow open access to anyone in the world.

---

[1]https://www.gartner.com/en/newsroom/press-releases/2018-05-03-gartner-survey-reveals-the-scarcity-of-current-blockchain-developments.

In other words, anyone can submit and access the transactions and participate in the consensus protocols. (2) Consortium blockchains restrict the consensus protocols to a pre-selected set of nodes, i.e., across multiple organizations. However, submission of and access to the transactions can be either public or limited to a group of participants. (3) Private blockchains are governed by a single organization that decides about the participants' permissions to submit/read transactions [15].

Public blockchains are also known as "permissionless" because they are open and decentralized. Besides, there is no central party that can add or remove members from the network. The full distribution of the transactions among untrusted nodes guarantees that it is almost impossible to tamper with the system. Characteristics like public verifiability, transparency, and integrity to prevent unauthorized modifications make these blockchains very powerful in the presence of untrusted participants. However, these networks have performance problems, as the transaction throughput is limited, and the latency is high as a result of the mining process [16].

In consortium and private blockchains, also called "permissioned," a central authority decides on the rights of the participants in the network. These blockchains require fewer validators than the "permissionless" ones what makes them more efficient. Similarly, "permissioned" blockchains offer more privacy and reduce redundancy as they have less data replication. However, they may be susceptible to trust issues, given that they are partially centralized. For example, the network can be tampered with if a majority of the organizations in the consortium agree to it [16].

Caterpillar relies on a public blockchain, specifically Ethereum,[2] so that the system assumes an environment in which no trust among the process participants is required. However, the design principles promoted by Caterpillar could be applied and adapted to consortium/private blockchains depending on the level of trust existing among the process participants.

3.3 Executing Blockchain-Based Collaborative Business Processes: Challenges and Principles

Blockchain offers a transparent and cryptographically secured environment built on consensus within a distributed peer-to-peer network. This closed and complex ecosystem opens a broad range of opportunities to perform collaborative processes, but it also introduces some crucial challenges. Among those, the amount of computational power and data storage capabilities are limited. Thus, when implementing blockchain-based processes, a critical decision relies on which data/operations must be stored/performed in the blockchain (i.e., on-chain) and which outside of the blockchain (i.e., off-chain) [3]. As such, several operations on collaborative

---

[2]https://ethereum.org/en/.

processes rely on data stored off-chain. However, there is no guarantee about the integrity of off-chain transactions, e.g., they can be compromised in the presence of unknown or untrusted sources. Therefore, the participants would need to collaboratively assert the off-chain decisions before proceeding with the execution on-chain.

3.3.1   Choreographies Versus Single-Pool Process Models

Several existing works use choreographies and collaboration diagrams to design and execute collaborative business processes [9]. A choreography diagram captures how the participants in a collaborative process interact, i.e., the possible interaction sequences. Choreography diagrams are intended to capture situations where "there is no central controller, responsible entity, or observer" [11]. Still, in our setting, the blockchain and the smart contracts it hosts conceptually play the role of a coordination mechanism. The focus of a choreography is not the orchestration of a process but to capture the participants' behavior based on the messages they sent and receive. In blockchain environments, participants share a common infrastructure, i.e., the blockchain, which acts as an orchestrator. Indeed, the blockchain specificity hides the organizational separation modeled as BPMN pools in the standard, typically implemented through different systems.

A drawback of blockchain platforms is that smart contracts cannot invoke/interact with operations executed off-chain [3]. The latter hinders the notion of message exchanges when implementing collaborative processes. For example, a participant sending a message to another means writing a transaction in the blockchain. The receiver can read the message, but also the other participants with access to a node in the network, i.e., everyone in public blockchains. Therefore, in practice, interactions between participants in blockchain environments do not necessarily materialize as message exchanges, but rather as transactions executed on-chain.

Aligned with the above, Caterpillar uses process diagrams with a single pool: it can represent the business process, and it makes use of blockchain for data storage, computation, and communication. This decision does not contradict the standard definition of collaboration and choreography diagrams. Over time, both single-pool models and collaborative/choreography models have been used to capture collaborative processes. For example, two of the earlier approaches to collaborative process modeling and execution were the Mentor and the Self-Serv systems, which relied on single-pool models, represented as statecharts (Mentor in the context of independent organizational units in an enterprise, and Self-Serv in an inter-organizational setting) [1, 14]. Indeed, choreographies can be translated into executable processes shared by all the parties. In our approach, each organization still maintains its internal processes running off-chain, sharing on-chain only the parts of the process relevant to the collaboration as for choreography diagrams. The critical difference in our proposal is that, as the participants must write transactions in the blockchain, we replace the message exchanges by the execution of tasks, which in our opinion, are more convenient in blockchain settings. Also, by representing the collaboration as a single process, we can include constructions like sub-processes and event propagation, which increases the process reusability and offers a broader range of options to the participants on the execution.

3.3.2 Compiled Versus Interpreted

Existing approaches primarily compile high-level process models into smart contracts to be deployed and executed on a blockchain platform. In these compiled approaches, each element in the process model is statically encoded as a set of instructions embedded into the smart contract. For example, consider a simple process model with one start event followed by a task whose execution enables an end event. In a compiled approach, the derived smart contract code would contain three blocks of fixed instructions, i.e., implementing each element's execution logic. This approach exploits immutability as a source of trust. Once deployed in the blockchain, the code of the smart contract is immutable. Thus, no participant can modify the process execution to their benefit. However, this comes at the cost of inflexibility. In other words, a minor change in the model entails generating and deploying new smart contracts. Also, active process instances, started before updating the model, remain tied to the contracts' old version.

Compiled approaches may also lead to efficiency issues on the deployment costs, i.e., resulting from deploying each newly generated contract. Besides, they may be redundant as they commonly repeat instructions in processes sharing a similar structure. In public blockchain platforms like Ethereum, the deployment costs are proportional to the contract size, i.e., the smallest, the best. For example, a process model with two script tasks may lead to two similar blocks of instructions since both activities share the same execution logic. However, these efficiency limitations mainly apply to blockchain platforms in which participants must pay for deploying a transaction. In blockchain platforms not tied to cryptocurrencies, such as Hyperledger,[3] deploying the smart contracts incurs no fee. Thus, the increase in the contract's size due to repeated instructions is not a significant issue.

In contrast, an interpreted execution of processes relying on data can prevent issues related to flexibility and deployment costs. For example, instead of being encoded as fixed blocks of instructions, the information about each element in a process model can be stored in a generic data structure. Indeed, each process perspective would require different data structures, i.e., control-flow, data, and resource. Then, participants may add, update, or remove elements during the process execution, supporting a more flexible implementation. A singleton smart contract (the interpreter) encodes the modeling language's semantics from the corresponding process data and can execute a given process model. Hence, the

---

[3]https://www.hyperledger.org/.

interpreter combined with the data structures approach reduces the deployment costs, i.e., an update of the process model would require a local update of the data structure and not redeploy the entire smart contract. For example, consider a process model that has an event. Accordingly, the control-flow data structure stores its type, incoming, and outgoing arcs information (i.e., they can be encoded using compact bitsets). Then, to trigger the event, the interpreter would query the control-flow data structure and perform the operations as defined in the BPMN standard. Therefore, in contrast to compiled approaches, no matter how many events are in the model, only one block of instructions to execute them is required.

Contrary to traditional programming languages in which interpreted solutions are less efficient, in public blockchain platforms, the size of the code and deployment costs play a predominant role in the total costs of executing smart contracts. Thus efficiency mostly depends on these parameters, and an interpreted approach reduces both the code size and the deployment costs compared to compiled solutions.

However, the flexibility of interpreted approaches may lead to trust issues or inconsistencies during the execution of the processes. For example, to avoid a participant trying to take advantage of updating the process at runtime (not possible in compiled approaches), the other participants require a more sophisticated control mechanism to prevent that behavior. Besides, adding, updating, or removing elements at runtime may lead to deadlocks if not performed correctly. None of the two issues above is present in compiled approaches.

In summary, there is a trade-off between whether to use compiled or interpreted approaches in the process execution. Compiled strategies seem more suitable in scenarios in which flexibility is not a requirement or in blockchain platforms where the participants pay no fee to deploy the contracts. In contrast, interpreted solutions fit better for processes subject to changes at runtime or executed on public blockchains where the participants must pay a transaction fee. Accordingly, the Caterpillar system provides two engines, i.e., compilation-based and interpretation-based, so the participants can decide based on their requirements which approach fits better.

3.4 Overview of the Caterpillar System

The BPMN models in Figs. 3.1, 3.2, 3.3, 3.4 and 3.5 provide an overview of the Caterpillar system. First, any collaborative process participant designs the joint BPMN model, serving as an agreement among them (as shown in Fig. 3.1). Then, the same or another participant uses Caterpillar to transform the corresponding model into smart contracts, which later will enforce the execution of the process instances. Note that none of the participants needs to run a blockchain node. Instead, they will connect/interact with a blockchain network through Caterpillar, i.e., participants can also decide in which network they want to deploy the contracts.

To produce the smart contracts from the process models, Fig. 3.2 illustrates how the participant can choose either the compilation-based or interpretation-

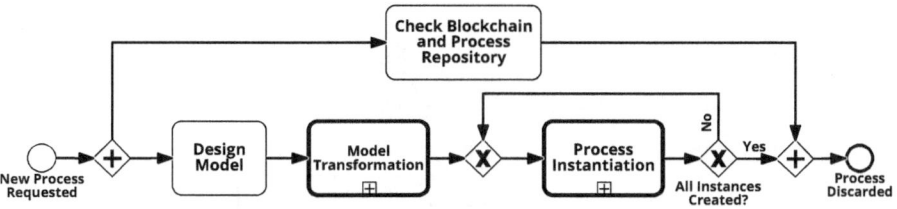

Fig. 3.1 Overview of a process execution on caterpillar

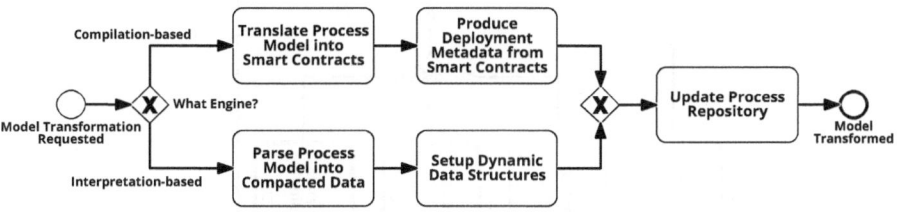

Fig. 3.2 Sub-process: model transformation, from BPMN models to smart contracts

based engines for the process execution (see [6] and [7] for further details). Then, Caterpillar stores all the metadata regarding the process transformation in a decentralized process repository (off-chain) shared by all the participants. Note that each participant can check the information from the process repository and the blockchain at any time. Besides, once transformed, the generated artifacts can be used to create as many process instances as required (Fig. 3.1).

To create new process instances (Fig. 3.3), a participant, referred to as case creator, may use Caterpillar's user interfaces or create the instances directly through the blockchain, i.e., using the metadata produced either from the compilation or the parsing of the model. The blockchain address produced when the transaction is mined will serve as the process instance's identifier. Then, during the execution of a process instance, the participants have different options: bind actors to roles dynamically, update the current process instance's control-flow, or execute tasks allocated as work-items. Indeed, participants can verify the state of the process at any time and execute allocated tasks only when enabled in the control-flow.[4] Also, to execute a task, a participant can retrieve and send data to the blockchain, i.e., check-out and check-in operations from user tasks in the BPMN model [2].

Although compilation-based solutions are less flexible than interpretation-based ones, Caterpillar allows some flexibility for compilation-based approaches, achieved through late-binding and late-modeling of processes [13], i.e., flexibility by loose-ness [12]. Both the compilation-based and interpretation-based engines of Cater-

---

[4]Note that participants can directly interact with contracts deployed by Caterpillar in the blockchain without using the user interface of Caterpillar. In other words, they can implement their off-chain components to handle the blockchain interactions if they prefer.

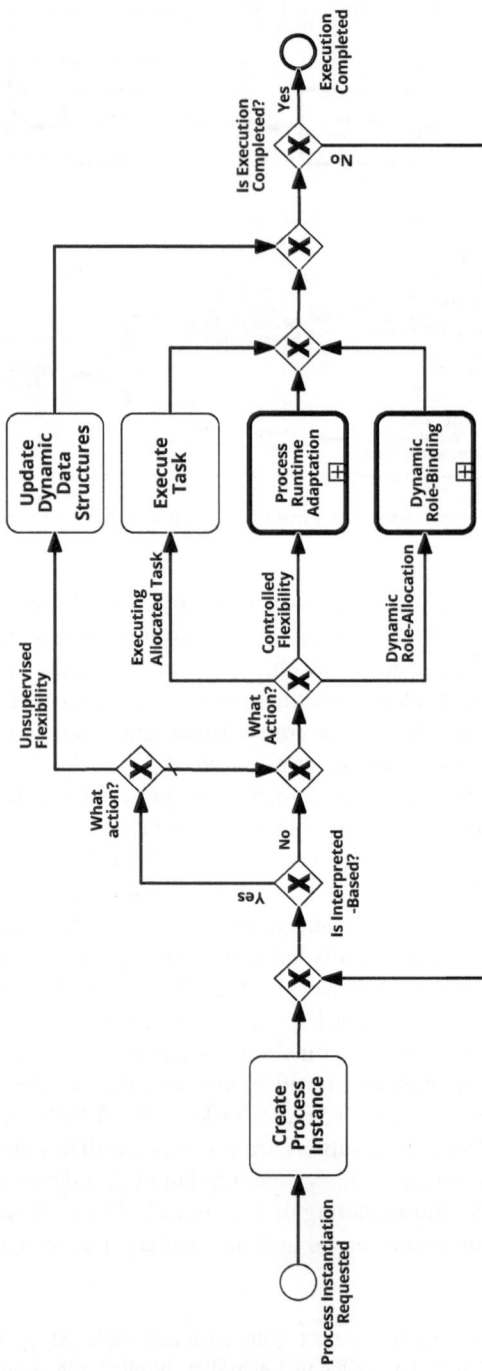

Fig. 3.3 Sub-process: process instantiation, creation, and execution of process instances

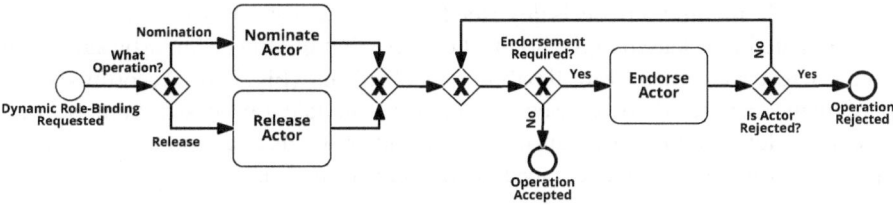

Fig. 3.4 Sub-process: dynamic role-binding, allocating actors to roles at runtime

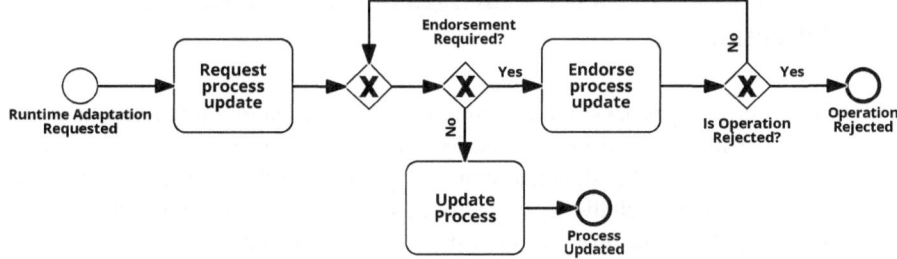

Fig. 3.5 Sub-process: process runtime adaptation, controlled flexibility on the control-flow

pillar allow linking call-activities to smart contract instances implementing the corresponding sub-processes during the execution. Accordingly, Caterpillar introduces agreement policies to handle flexibility by looseness mechanisms, which do not introduce deadlocks and without requiring additional verification techniques to be put into place. These mechanisms, labeled as controlled flexibility in Fig. 3.3, are further discussed in references [5, 8].

Other flexibility mechanisms, such as adding, skipping, or removing elements in the process model, are possible only for the interpretation-based engine. For example, according to the taxonomy presented in [12], there are four major control-flow-based flexibility requirements: adaptation, evolution, variability, and looseness. In that regard, the interpretation-based engine supports those four requirements. However, the adaptation, evolution, and variability requirements, labeled as unsupervised flexibility in Fig. 3.3, may lead to deadlocks in the interpretation-based engine. Thus, such updates on the interpreter's dynamic data structure could be performed at runtime if and only if all the participants agree on it as they entail a higher risk to tamper with the process execution. More specifically, process participants should verify off-chain whether those unsupervised changes are consistent before propagating them to the blockchain. To that end, participants can either perform the consistency validation automatically (by using private-owned tools) or manually.

Figures 3.4–3.5 outline how participants can enforce the flexibility mechanisms by consensus (see [5, 8]). First, participants can nominate or release actors into roles during the process execution, subject to other participants' endorsement. For example, after creating a process instance, the case creator can appoint an actor to play a role in that instance and to execute the tasks granted to that role. The dynamic role-binding schema is described by policies, restricting how the actors can be nominated or released and who must endorse that binding. Similarly, agreement policies restrict control-flow flexibility mechanisms (Fig. 3.5). Accordingly, the participants can decide by consensus whether to update a process at runtime, e.g., to enforce late-binding of a sub-process. In other words, Caterpillar promotes an approach of flexibility by underspecification [13] or looseness [12].

3.5 Caterpillar's Open Challenges and Future Research Directions

Caterpillar represents process data as code snippets written in the Solidity language and embedded in the process models. Further research needs to focus on high-level representations of the data and conditions for blockchain-based collaborative processes. Among the challenges regarding data access and representation, for example, encrypted data provides confidentiality, but it reduces enforceability of the process as no operation can be performed with such data. This trade-off between privacy and enforceability becomes even more critical in the presence of dynamic scenarios. In such cases, the process participants must reach consensus at runtime about how and by whom the process data can be accessed/updated. Other challenges come when deciding how to share data among participants selectively and when performing trusted operations on private data, under the performance and scalability limitations of the blockchains. Besides, the immutability of the transactions in the blockchain may introduce issues when revoking privileges. For example, process participants may have access to encrypted data forever once they own the decryption key, even after leaving the organization. Designing models for shared data to overcome the latest challenges is a venue for further research.

Caterpillar allows participants to update a process model dynamically. It raises the question of how to ensure that the already-running instances do not end up in an inconsistent state after a process model change. A direction for future work is to adapt existing approaches for consistency verification of dynamic process model changes to this setting [12]. Similarly, the verification and monitoring of blockchain-based processes and the applicability of process mining techniques mostly remains an unexplored research area. Although some nascent works already extract event logs for process mining from the blockchain [4, 10], they are mainly platform-dependent. Thus, further research is still required.

The current version of Caterpillar is built on Ethereum, i.e., a public blockchain, which may introduce scalability issues. Consortium blockchain technologies such as Hyperledger and other blockchain architectures that support much higher throughput can offer higher scalability. Thus, studying the Caterpillar approach on different blockchain platforms and configurations is a direction for future work. Similarly, the Caterpillar system's portability requires further research to allow collaborative processes to be executed across multiple blockchain platforms.

Acknowledgments This chapter summarized the research works presented in the papers [5–8]. For the full specification of the Caterpillar system, we refer the reader to the corresponding papers and the code repository of Caterpillar: https://github.com/orlenyslp/Caterpillar. Many thanks to my Ph.D. supervisors Prof. Marlon Dumas and Prof. Luciano García Bañuelos, and co-author Prof. Ingo Weber, for their valuable advice and guidance.

References

1. Benatallah, B., Sheng, Q.Z., Ngu, A.H.H., Dumas, M.: Declarative composition and peer-to-peer provisioning of dynamic web services. In: Proceedings of the 18th International Conference on Data Engineering, San Jose, CA, USA, February 26 - March 1, 2002, pp. 297–308 (2002). https://doi.org/10.1109/ICDE.2002.994738
2. Dumas, M., Rosa, M.L., Mendling, J., Reijers, H.A.: Fundamentals of Business Process Management, 2nd edn. Springer, Berlin (2018). https://doi.org/10.1007/978-3-662-56509-4
3. Eberhardt, J., Tai, S.: On or off the blockchain? insights on off-chaining computation and data. In: Proceedings of the Service-Oriented and Cloud Computing - 6th IFIP WG 2.14 European Conference, ESOCC 2017, Oslo, September 27–29, 2017, pp. 3–15 (2017). https://doi.org/10.1007/978-3-319-67262-5_1
4. Klinkmüller, C., Ponomarev, A., Tran, A.B., Weber, I., van der Aalst, W.M.: Mining blockchain processes: Extracting process mining data from blockchain applications. In: Proceedings of the Business Process Management: Blockchain and Central and Eastern Europe Forum - BPM 2019 Blockchain and CEE Forum, Vienna, September 1–6, 2019, pp. 71–86 (2019). https://doi.org/10.1007/978-3-030-30429-4_6
5. López-Pintado, O., Dumas, M., García-Bañuelos, L., Weber, I.: Dynamic role binding in blockchain-based collaborative business processes. In: Proceedings of the Advanced Information Systems Engineering - 31st International Conference, CAiSE 2019, Rome, June 3–7, 2019, pp. 399–414 (2019). https://doi.org/10.1007/978-3-030-21290-2_25
6. López-Pintado, O., Dumas, M., García-Bañuelos, L., Weber, I.: Interpreted execution of business process models on blockchain. In: 23rd IEEE International Enterprise Distributed Object Computing Conference, EDOC 2019, Paris, October 28–31, 2019, pp. 206–215 (2019). https://doi.org/10.1109/EDOC.2019.00033
7. López-Pintado, O., García-Bañuelos, L., Dumas, M., Weber, I., Ponomarev, A.: Caterpillar: a business process execution engine on the Ethereum blockchain. Softw. Pract. Exper. **49**(7), 1162–1193 (2019)
8. López-Pintado, O., Dumas, M., García-Bañuelos, L., Weber, I.: Controlled flexibility in blockchain-based collaborative business processes. Inf. Syst. 101622 (2020). https://doi.org/10.1016/j.is.2020.101622
9. Mendling, J., et. al.: Blockchains for business process management - challenges and opportunities. ACM Trans. Manag. Inf. Syst. **9**(1), 4:1–4:16 (2018). https://doi.org/10.1145/3183367
10. Mühlberger, R., Bachhofner, S., Di Ciccio, C., García-Bañuelos, L., López-Pintado, O.: Extracting event logs for process mining from data stored on the blockchain. In: Business Process Management Workshops - BPM 2019 International Workshops, Vienna, September 1–6, 2019, Revised Selected Papers, pp. 690–703 (2019). https://doi.org/10.1007/978-3-030-37453-2_55
11. Object Management Group: Business process model and notation (2014). https://www.omg.org/spec/BPMN/2.0.2
12. Reichert, M., Weber, B.: Enabling Flexibility in Process-Aware Information Systems - Challenges, Methods, Technologies. Springer, Berlin (2012). https://doi.org/10.1007/978-3-642-30409-5

13. Schonenberg, H., Mans, R., Russell, N., Mulyar, N., van der Aalst, W.M.: Towards a taxonomy of process flexibility. In: Proceedings of the Forum at the CAiSE'08 Conference, Montpellier, June 18–20, 2008, pp. 81–84 (2008)
14. Wodtke, D., Weißenfels, J., Weikum, G., Dittrich, A.K.: The mentor project: Steps toward enterprise-wide workflow management. In: Proceedings of the Twelfth International Conference on Data Engineering, February 26 - March 1, 1996, New Orleans, Louisiana, pp. 556–565 (1996). https://doi.org/10.1109/ICDE.1996.492206
15. Xu, X., Weber, I., Staples, M.: Architecture for Blockchain Applications. Springer, Berlin (2019). https://doi.org/10.1007/978-3-030-03035-3
16. Zheng, Z., Xie, S., Dai, H., Chen, X., Wang, H.: Blockchain challenges and opportunities: a survey. IJWGS **14**(4), 352–375 (2018). https://doi.org/10.1504/IJWGS.2018.10016848

Chapter 4
Executing DMN Decisions
on the Blockchain

Stephan Haarmann

Abstract Collaborations of organizations are based on contracts, which must
be interpreted and thus leave room for misunderstandings. Collaborators have
to reach a shared understanding of their contract and must trust one another.
Blockchain technologies in general and especially smart contracts promise unam-
biguous enforceable contracts and can act as a neutral and trusted source of truth.
This chapter presents two methods to encode decisions as smart contracts. The first
orchestrates the decision-making process and executes the decision logic as specified. The second orchestrates the decision-making in a privacy-preserving manner
and allows semi-automated conflict resolution. In both methods, the Blockchain has
the role of a neutral third party, of a single source of truth, to which all collaborators
can be held accountable.

4.1 Introduction

Blockchain technologies have a wide range of applications and the potential to
innovate how organizations operate. The technologies can be used to record proofs
of actions, for example, for supply chain monitoring. They can embed and run
executable code, called smart contracts, e.g., to mediate and orchestrate actions
in business processes [6, 7, 11]. Blockchains' unique properties allow monitoring,
executing, and orchestrating collaborations in settings of limited trust.

A legal contract defines conditions under which certain parties have specific
obligations. In business process models [8], obligations are expressed by activities
and conditions are encoded in the control flow, which limits the ordering of
activities [5]. Using smart contracts, we can represent activities as callable functions
and enforce the control flow. However, many legal contracts and processes contain
data conditions and data-based decisions, e.g., to realize conditional branching.

S. Haarmann (✉)
Group Business Process Technology, Hasso Plattner Institute, University of Potsdam, Potsdam,
Germany
e-mail: stephan.haarmann@hpi.de

© The Author(s), under exclusive license to Springer Nature Switzerland AG 2021   43
A. Koschmider, S. Schulte (eds.), *Blockchain and Robotic Process Automation*,
https://doi.org/10.1007/978-3-030-81409-0_4

Here, a decision consists of data-based rules and derives a data output for given inputs.

In this chapter, we show that data-based decisions, which may be part of legal contracts, can be executed in a transparent and tamper-prove manner using blockchain technology. Therefore, we map decisions modeled using Decision Model and Notation (DMN) [9] to smart contracts, which collect and store data inputs from different participants, execute decisions, and communicate the outcome. Furthermore, we discuss the risks involved when publishing data to a blockchain and propose a solution that monitors decisions without disclosure of sensitive data but with the capability of resolving conflicts.

This chapter is structured as follows. In the next section, we briefly introduce the DMN standard and an example used during the reminder of the chapter (Sect. 4.2). Section 4.3 presents the translation of DMN models to smart contracts. Next, we discuss privacy requirements and sketch a privacy-preserving implementation (Sect. 4.4). We discuss and conclude the chapter in Sect. 4.5.

4.2   Motivating Example Using Decision Model and Notation

Contracts and other written documents are usually ambiguous. However, when a smart contract is created, ambiguity needs to be removed. Furthermore, it is important that all participants share a common understanding since, once deployed, the smart contract becomes binding. In case of business processes and decisions, standards have been proposed to capture and communicate the logic clearly.

The DMN standard [9] is both a standardized modeling language and an exchange format for decision models. A full DMN decision model contains two layers: a logic layer comprising rules and a requirements level describing which inputs and sub-decisions are required by each decision.

The *requirements layer* defines decisions and required inputs. Inputs can be either provided directly (called *data inputs*) or derived from sub-decisions. Visually, requirements are depicted in an acyclic, directed graph. A vertex in the graph is either a decision represented by a rectangle or a data input visualized by a rounded shape.[1] Arcs depict dependencies: a decision requires all data inputs and all outputs of sub-decisions from which an arc leads to said decision.

For illustration, consider a furniture retailer and a logistics provider. The companies have a service level agreement: if the logistics provider ships deliveries incomplete or delayed, it must compensate the furniture retailer. The example decision requirements diagram is depicted in Fig. 4.1. It comprises two decisions: Service Level and Penal Damage. The furniture company's service level depends on two inputs: the number of years it ships products with the logistic provider and the number of shipments in the past six months. The decision derives

---

[1]DMN supports further elements, which we do not use.

Fig. 4.1 The decision requirements graph for the service level agreement example. Data inputs are rounded. Decisions are rectangles

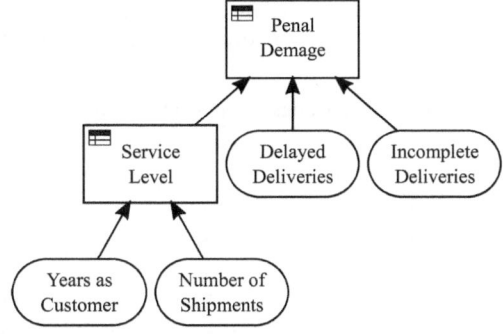

Table 4.1 Decision table for the decision `Service Level` with six rules

U	Inputs		Outputs
	Years as customer	Number of shipments	Service level
1	*int*	*int*	{*Silver, Gold, Platinum*}
2	≤ 1	—	Silver
3	∈ (1, 5]	≤ 10,000	Silver
4	∈ (1, 5]	> 10,000	Gold
5	> 5	≤ 5000	Gold
6	> 5	> 5000	Gold

a service level that is used in combination with the ratios of delayed and incomplete deliveries to retrieve the penal damage. The logistic provider must pay the damage to the retailer.

The decision requirements describe the decisions and their required inputs. However, it is not defined how a particular decision is made. The logic layer defines the rules of each decision. While different formal and informal specifications are possible, we are interested in a precise definition of the decision logic. In this chapter, we consider decision tables because they are widely adopted by industry, expressive, and formally defined. In a mathematical sense, a decision is a function mapping a combination of inputs to an output. A decision table describes such a function by a list of rules and a hit policy that defines how the rules are evaluated.

The example has two decisions and two decision tables, respectively. The first decision table (Table 4.1) describes the decision `Service Level`. The second decision table (Table 4.2) specifies the rules to derive the `Penal Damage`. Table 4.1 comprises six rules all evaluated according to the *unique* hit policy (U in the top left corner). This means that rules do not overlap: for each possible combination of inputs exists one and only one matching rule. The conditions of each rule are specified in the second and third column, while the output is given in the last one. The second decision table has nine rules and the hit policy *first* (F in the top left corner). This means that multiple rules can match a given input combination, but the rules are always evaluated sequentially, from top to bottom. When a rule matches,

Table 4.2 Decision table for the `Penal Damage`. The inputs `Delayed Deliveries` and `Incomplete Deliveries` as well as the output are integers specifying percentages

F	Inputs			Outputs
	Delayed deliveries	Incomplete deliveries	Service level	Penal damage
1	*int*	*int*	{*Silver, Gold, Platinum*}	*int*
2	= 0	= 0	—	0
3	< 3	< 3	∈ {Silver,Gold}	0
4	< 3	< 3	Platinum	5
5	< 5	< 5	Silver	0
6	< 5	< 5	Gold	5
7	≥ 5	≥ 5	Silver	5
8	≥ 5	≥ 5	Gold	10
9	—	—	Platinum	20

its output is produced and the evaluation terminates. In general, every decision table can be transformed into a unique one [1].

While we only look at decisions in this chapter, a decision can be embedded in a business process such as the ones mentioned in earlier chapters of this book. A decision can be used to update variables or to realize conditional control flow (e.g., exclusive gateways).

4.3 Translating Decisions to Smart Contracts

Blockchains are useful in collaborative settings with limited trust. In collaborative decisions, required data inputs may be provided by multiple participants and outcomes may be of interest to various parties. Furthermore, both the data provision and decision invocation may be restricted to certain parties. From this setting, we derive the following requirements for corresponding smart contracts:

RQ1 Confirmability: inputs and outputs must be stored transparently, so all participants can comprehend the decision and confirm the result.

RQ2 Access Control: write access to the smart contract must be limited to prevent third parties from manipulating the decision.

RQ3 Tamper Protection: the rules must be executable and tamper-prove. When the decision output is calculated on-chain, participants can trust the result as long as they trust the inputs.

From requirements RQ1–RQ3, additional more detailed ones can be derived. Access Control (RQ2) can be performed on a per-attribute level, and the decision may be invoked automatically to avoid unnecessary blockchain transactions. Furthermore, data inputs and outputs should be easily accessible.

RQ4 Attribute-Level Access Control: only specific parties can update an attribute reflecting possible obligations and rights specified in the contract.

RQ5   Automatic Execution: a decision is made when its requirements are satisfied.
RQ6   Accessibility: outcomes are logged and accessible to all participants. This
        establishes transparency as any participant can view and confirm the result.
        It also eases the integration into an off-chain system.

The requirements address both static and behavioral aspects of smart contract imple-
mentation. We consider Ethereum smart contracts that are written using Solidity.
First, we need to collect inputs. Therefore, we create a smart contract, called
StateContract (cf. Listing 4.1), with an attribute for each input and output.
We include outputs since they can be inputs for another decision. Furthermore, we
add corresponding setter functions.

According to RQ2 and RQ4, access to these setters must be limited. The smart
contract stores for each participant the attributes that they may set. This information
is stored cost-efficiently using bitmaps, where a bit corresponds to a specific
attribute. When participants call a setter, the contract checks whether they may set
the attribute. Furthermore, attributes should not be updated once they have been
set since this may invalidate already executed decisions. Therefore, we store an
additional bitmap which is updated whenever an attribute is set. An attribute can
only be set if the corresponding bit has the value 0.

Listing 4.1 The StateContract, which stores inputs and outputs, manages access rights, and
tracks the current state

```
1    contract StateContract is withRightManagement {
2
3        // input data
4        uint8 public yearsAsCustomer;
5        uint32 public numberOfShipments;
6        uint32 public numberDelayedShipments;
7        uint8 public numberIncompleteShipments;
8        // outputs
9        uint8 public penalDamage;
10       uint8 public serviceLevel;
11       // access rights
12       DecisionServiceLevel public decisionSla;
13       DecisionPenalDamage public decisionDamage;
14       // state information
15       uint8 public state;
16       // Setters
17       ...
18   }
```

Requirements RQ3, RQ5, and RQ6 address the decision logic. Since a decision is
basically a function, the outcome depends only on the data inputs. If we split the
storage of the data inputs and decision outputs from the execution of the decision
logic, we can reuse the logic and reduce the cost for storing and executing the
decision logic. Therefore, we add a smart contract dedicated to the decision logic.
This so-called *decision contract* (cf. Listing 4.2) comprises two things: a function
evaluating the logic of a decision for given inputs and a log recording the outcome.

The function, which for reasons of simplicity is called "decide," consists of three phases. First, all required inputs are retrieved from the data contract (l. 6). Additionally, a variable is declared to store the output (l. 7). In the second phase, the logic is evaluated (l. 9ff). For the unique and first-hit policies, sequential if-else-if statements are used. Each conditional branch represents one rule. Within one of the branches, the output variable is set to the output of the corresponding rule (see l. 10). In the final phase, the output is both stored in the data contract (l. 14) and logged (l. 15). The log entry contains the outcome as well as a reference to the data contract. The latter can be used as a correlation key and filter criteria for the participants.

Listing 4.2 The `DecisionServiceLevel` encoding and executing the decision logic of the sub-decision service level

```
1   contract DecisionServiceLevel {
2       event ServiceLevel(address instance, uint8 serviceLevel)
3
4       function decide(address _address) external {
5           // retrieving the state
6           StateContract state = StateContract(address);
7           uint8 serviceLevelResult;
8           // verifying rules
9           if (state.yearsAsCustomer() <= 1) {
10              serviceLevelResult = 0; // Silver
11          }
12          ...
13          // persisting and logging the result
14          state.setServiceLevel(serviceLevelResult);
15          ServiceLevel(state, serviceLevelResult);
16      }
17  }
```

The translation of DMN models to Solidity smart contracts has been explained in more detail in [3]. This implementation stores data and executes decision logic transparently and tamper-prove. This is achieved by storing all information publicly on the blockchain. Especially public blockchains would enable arbitrary parties to access this information. This can be problematic because contracts often contain sensitive data that must not be disclosed.

4.4 Privacy-Preserving Decision-Making

In this section, we present a solution that enables blockchain support for decisions without revealing sensitive information. Figure 4.2 provides an overview of the necessary steps. We employ cryptography to find agreement on decision models, inputs, and outputs. Conflicts regarding the outputs can be detected on the concealed data. Then, the smart contract can resolve the conflicts among participants at the cost of revealing the data similar to a legal contract that gets enforced at court if proofs are provided.

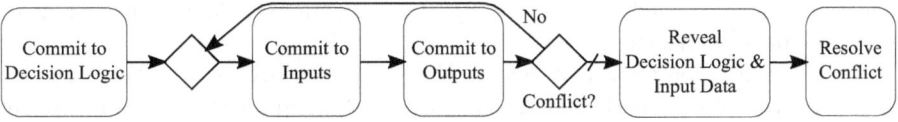

Fig. 4.2 The steps of the privacy-preserving decision-making: commitments do not reveal any data but can be used for conflict resolution

4.4.1 Cryptographic Preliminaries

First, we present cryptographic concepts that we use. For details, see pertinent literature, such as [2].

A *hash function* maps a value from one domain to another. A cryptographic hash function has the following properties: (1) the function is collision free, (2) it is practically irreversible, and (3) calculating a hash is feasible.

A *cryptographic signature scheme* in asymmetric encryption consists of two functions. The first function creates a *signature* given a value and a private key. The second function verifies a given *signature* using a public key and a value. It should be computationally infeasible to derive a valid signature without a private key. In blockchains, transactions are signed by the sending party.

A *commitment scheme* allows participants to commit publicly to a value without revealing it. Once the value has been disclosed, it can be aligned with the commitment. Therefore, a one-way function, for example, a cryptographic hash function, is required. To commit to a value, a participant hashes the value and publishes the hash. When the value is revealed, it can be hashed again to verify the commitment.

4.4.2 3-Phase Collaborative Decision-Making

With the help of the introduced cryptographic functions, we propose the following three-phase approach. First, participants commit to a decision model using a cryptographic hash function. The commitments of all participants must be the same to prove the common understanding of the decision model. In the second phase, all participants first commit to the same inputs and then to outputs. If the commitments of all participants are the same, further decisions can be executed by repeating phase two. If the commitments indicate conflicting outputs, the conflict can automatically be resolved given that the true inputs and logic are provided. Since the participants agreed on both, any participant has the necessary knowledge. The smart contract can interpret the decision logic for the given inputs, derive the outputs, hash them, and compare the hashes to the given commitments. Those commitments that match the hashed outputs are correct. The others are incorrect and violate the contract. The violations can be treated accordingly, e.g., by punishing fraudulent participants or enforcing the right decision.

Since the decision logic is provided when a conflict occurs, we cannot encode them directly into a smart contract, and we must interpret the decision instead. Without loss of generality, we assume that every decision table has the hit policy *unique* [1]. We store the scheme of the decision table, which allows interpreting the values semantically. DMN's S-FEEL expression language supports comparing values using equality, inequality, greater than and smaller than operators. For numeric values, these operations can be translated into intervals. An interval can be expressed using four variables. Two to represent the lower-bound and two for the upper bound. Each bound is represented by a number for the bound and a Boolean indicating whether the bound is inclusive or exclusive. To interpret the condition, we only need to check whether the input lies within the specified bounds. String, Boolean, and enumerate domains can only be checked for equality or inequality, which is straight forward. To check a rule, we iterate over inputs and conditions while evaluating the expression in each cell. To check a full table, we iterate over all rules until one matches.

However, many blockchains limit the computations per transactions. We can use continuations [10] to overcome this limitation: for each call, we return or store the last rule that has been fully evaluated. The next call can continue with the evaluation of the next rule.

Conflicts in our approach are expensive: not only does it require many transactions and computations to resolve a conflict, but it also reveals the sensitive decision logic and inputs. We can improve this approach further by embedding an incentive mechanism that discourages malicious behavior. The mechanism uses cryptocurrencies, which are a central aspect of most modern blockchains. Using escrows managed by the smart contract, we can punish fraud and compensate honesty. Whenever a conflict is reported, the escrows of the fraudulent parties are depleted to compensate honest parties. In a well-tuned incentive mechanism, the potential punishment outweighs the possible gain for fraudsters and the compensation outweighs the damage done to honest participants. Consequently, frauds are not lucrative and should not occur at all. For more details on the approach in this section, we refer to [4].

4.4.3   Example Walkthrough

Consider the scenario of the logistics provider and furniture retailer introduced before. Assuming that the logistics provider negotiates the service level agreement with every customer individually publishing them would put the provider at a disadvantage for future negotiations; hence, the parties decide to use the privacy-preserving variant introduced in this section.

The logistics provider and retailer negotiate the contract, create the decision model, and deploy the smart contract. Next, each participant hashes the model[2] and provides the hash to the smart contract. The smart contract compares the two hashes. If they are equal, the participants may continue, otherwise, they have to first find agreement on the hashes. Therefore, they should communicate the values and decide on one. Since the blockchain cannot know the real value, this conflict must be resolved manually.

During operation, both participants track the number of deliveries. If the retailer receives a customer complaint about a delivery being delayed or incomplete, the retailer records the information and communicates it to the logistics provider. The communication may happen on- or off-chain as long as it is secure and private.

At the end of every quarter, the penal damage is decided. At this point, both participants have all the data required by the decision. They hash this information and provide the hashes to the smart contract. If the hashes match, they may proceed with the decision by deriving the outputs off-chain. Once the participants have derived the output, they provide the hashes to the smart contract. Both the retailer and the logistics provider have to provide the output.

Once the smart contract receives the hashes, it compares them. If the hashes for the output conflict, the smart contract automatically starts the conflict resolution: participants can now provide the decision model and decision inputs. The smart contract will hash each one to verify the input by comparing the derived hash with the provided hash. If the input passes verification, the decision is interpreted and the outputs are hashed to check which of the provided hashes are wrong and which are correct. This knowledge can be used to penalize fraudsters and to compensate honest behavior. Assuming that the logistics provider lied on the penal damage they have to pay while the retailer was honest, the smart contract can punish the former and compensate the latter using funds from the logistics provider's escrow.

4.5 Conclusion

Organizations collaborate and specify the terms for collaborations in contracts. Many of these contracts contain decisions. For a successful collaboration, it is crucial that the parties have a common understanding of the decision logic and the data used, so they derive the same conclusions.

We presented a method to coordinate and monitor collaborative decisions transparently and tamper-prove. Therefore, we store all inputs and outputs on the blockchain and execute the decisions on-chain. However, this requires that all participants trust the blockchain network and that the data is not sensitive. Furthermore, this approach may introduce a delay since decisions have to be executed synchronously via multiple blockchain transactions. However, all participants

---

[2]All participants and the smart contract have to use the same hash function.

retrieve and operate on the same result, which removes the risk for conflicts and slow conflict resolution.

The second presented approach proves consent on the decision, its logic, and data, without the need for disclosing detailed information publicly. However, if participants disagree on the outcome of a decision, prior proofs can be used to resolve the conflict under disclosure of the data and logic. Additionally, we propose an incentive mechanism that makes some conflicts economically infeasible for all participants and may prevent frauds completely. The approach is limited to conflicts on the outputs and relies active participation of the involved parties (e.g., sharing data).

Our approaches are limited to decisions that can be expressed in DMN S-FEEL decision tables. However, some ideas can be generalized to arbitrary logic (as long as it is decidable). While blockchain technology offers advantages for collaborative decisions, these come at a cost. The synchronous nature may slow down collaborations, throughput is limited, and not all decisions can be publicly disclosed. Furthermore, our current approaches have no mechanism to deal with off-chain violations. In the future, blockchains may become valid proofs at court and/or consortia may vote on-chain on treating off-chain behavior.

References

1. Batoulis, K., Weske, M.: Disambiguation of DMN decision tables. In: Abramowicz, W., Paschke, A. (eds.) Proceedings of the Business Information Systems - 21st International Conference, BIS 2018, Berlin, July 18–20, 2018. Lecture Notes in Business Information Processing, vol. 320, pp. 236–249. Springer, Berlin (2018). https://doi.org/10.1007/978-3-319-93931-5_17
2. Goldreich, O.: The Foundations of Cryptography - Volume 1: Basic Techniques. Cambridge University Press, Cambridge (2001). https://doi.org/10.1017/CBO9780511546891. http://www.wisdom.weizmann.ac.il/%7Eoded/foc-vol1.html
3. Haarmann, S., Batoulis, K., Nikaj, A., Weske, M.: DMN decision execution on the ethereum blockchain. In: Krogstie, J., Reijers, H.A. (eds.) Proceedings of the Advanced Information Systems Engineering - 30th International Conference, CAiSE 2018, Tallinn, June 11–15, 2018. Lecture Notes in Computer Science, vol. 10816, pp. 327–341. Springer, Berlin (2018). https://doi.org/10.1007/978-3-319-91563-0_20
4. Haarmann, S., Batoulis, K., Nikaj, A., Weske, M.: Executing collaborative decisions confidentially on blockchains. In: Di Ciccio, C., Gabryelczyk, R., García-Bañuelos, L., Hernaus, T., Hull, R., Stemberger, M.I., Ko, A., Staples, M. (eds.) Proceedings of the Business Process Management: Blockchain and Central and Eastern Europe Forum - BPM 2019 Blockchain and CEE Forum, Vienna, September 1–6, 2019. Lecture Notes in Business Information Processing, vol. 361, pp. 119–135. Springer, Berlin (2019). https://doi.org/10.1007/978-3-030-30429-4_9
5. Ladleif, J., Weske, M.: A legal interpretation of choreography models. In: Francescomarino, C.D., Dijkman, R.M., Zdun, U. (eds.) Business Process Management Workshops - BPM 2019 International Workshops, Vienna, September 1–6, 2019. Revised Selected Papers. Lecture Notes in Business Information Processing, vol. 362, pp. 651–663. Springer, Berlin (2019). https://doi.org/10.1007/978-3-030-37453-2_52

6. Ladleif, J., Weske, M., Weber, I.: Modeling and enforcing blockchain-based choreographies. In: Hildebrandt, T.T., van Dongen, B.F., Röglinger, M., Mendling, J. (eds.) Proceedings of the Business Process Management - 17th International Conference, BPM 2019, Vienna, September 1–6, 2019. Lecture Notes in Computer Science, vol. 11675, pp. 69–85. Springer, Berlin (2019). https://doi.org/10.1007/978-3-030-26619-6_7
7. López-Pintado, O., García-Bañuelos, L., Dumas, M., Weber, I., Ponomarev, A.: Caterpillar: A business process execution engine on the ethereum blockchain. Softw. Pract. Exp. **49**(7), 1162–1193 (2019). https://doi.org/10.1002/spe.2702
8. Object Management Group: Business process model and notation (2014). https://www.omg.org/spec/BPMN/2.0.2
9. Object Management Group: Decision model and notation (2016). https://www.omg.org/spec/DMN/1.1/
10. Reynolds, J.C.: The discoveries of continuations. LISP Symb. Comput. **6**(3–4), 233–248 (1993)
11. Weber, I., Xu, X., Riveret, R., Governatori, G., Ponomarev, A., Mendling, J.: Untrusted business process monitoring and execution using blockchain. In: La Rosa, M., Loos, P., Pastor, O. (eds.) Proceedings of the Business Process Management - 14th International Conference, BPM 2016, Rio de Janeiro, September 18–22, 2016. Lecture Notes in Computer Science, vol. 9850, pp. 329–347. Springer, Berlin (2016). https://doi.org/10.1007/978-3-319-45348-4_19

Chapter 5
Dimo: Blockchain-Based Solution for Digital Payment

Florian Protschka

Abstract Mainly people in Africa do not have a bank account, which in turn opens the opportunities for criminal activities like theft and fraud. This does not stop the need people have to use money for consumption, but it does make it harder to send and receive it in a safe manner. To provide a solution, this chapter summarizes the blockchain-based digital payment platform *Dimo*. Dimo is a payment solution that is specifically for the people in Africa and starting in the countries of East Africa. Chainsulting is the developer, consultant in this project and the service provider for the local owner of the platform, who in turn works with the governments and central banks of the countries in which Dimo is active.

5.1 Introduction

Mainly people in Africa do not have a bank account, which in turn opens the opportunities for criminal activities like theft and fraud. There is simply no infrastructure to have and use bank accounts. People in Africa receive their salaries in cash and thus also keep their money in cash. All payment and any transfer of money will be made in cash. However, this does not stop the need people have to use money for consumption, but it does make it harder to send and receive it in a safe manner. It is common for the younger working population, who often moves to work in the cities, to send money to their older family members. Without a bank account, the cash is sent in envelopes or given to friends, which is not a secure solution. Additionally, in countries with not optimally functioning cash register systems, the ultimate result is that income is often not fully taxed. If people can only save money in cash, this means also that purchases mostly take place in cheap goods. The lack of a broad infrastructure for receiving and sending money may be inconceivable from the perspective of the first world. But this is the sad

F. Protschka (✉)
Chainsulting, Flensburg, Germany
e-mail: f.protschka@chainsulting.de

reality of millions of people in Africa. Because there is not a large-scale banking infrastructure, when customers mainly pay with cash companies must store it. They spend the purchase with external service providers or raw materials but also the salaries for employees in cash and that leads to uncertainties for all parties. Then the income from companies is difficult to understand, which is why tax evasion is a legitimate issue. Most of the large organizations have bank accounts, but with bank accounts lacking among regular citizens it becomes difficult to securely distribute donations to people or institutions, both in terms of the purely technical process and in terms of traceability.

What is needed is a (1) trust worthy third party and (2) a digital solution that is inexpensive or even free of charge for users. Referring to (1) such a third party (e.g., banks and notaries) does not exist for millions of people in Africa, which leads to uncertainty. Also, with respect to (2) a transparent, digital solution is missing that can be used without banking infrastructure. However, such digital solution must contain the official central bank money, because this is the only way to ensure legal security. At the same time, only the digital variant of central bank money leads to the broad masses of people understanding, for example regarding the value, and the companies are able to use it without any problems.

To provide a solution, the company Chainsulting[1] has developed the blockchain-based digital payment platform *Dimo*. The use of a Blockchain in such a scenario offers the possibilities to overcome widespread economic challenges, particularly where financial infrastructure is lacking. A blockchain solution offers access to financial institutions allowing financial transactions [1–3]. Dimo is able to solve issues for the everyday person all the way up to large corporations, despite the lack of infrastructure by better addressed and using their data securely and transparently.

This chapter is structured as follows. The next section summarizes Dimo. Subsequently a conclusion is presented.

5.2 Dimo: Blockchain-Based Solution

Dimo is a digital payment platform with which digital central bank money can be received and sent. At Dimo the blockchain technology ensures that digital central bank money can be used quickly, easily, and inexpensively. Users can use the digital money via their mobile device. The existence of this is based on the collaboration between Dimo, the governments, and central banks because Dimo is not a solution that was issued by the government or central bank, but a privately developed and published solution that cooperates with the state organization.

---

[1] https://chainsulting.de/.

5.2.1   Advantages of Dimo

The process for users is as follows. Users deposit their cash at local agents which can be retailers, hotels, cinemas, or independent providers. Then users receive this money from the agent, so the central bank money that they have previously paid in as cash, 1 to 1 as a digital variant on their Dimo account. The money can be received and sent via the Dimo app, the website, and Unstructured Supplementary Service Data (USSD).

A chat function is integrated in the Dimo app, which users can use to send the money directly to their relatives and friends, who they can save directly as contacts in the app. When paying, users can now use Dimo, so there is no longer a need for cash. They send the digital money as payment from their device to the recipient's device. No bank account or any other bank-like infrastructure is required for people to use the platform.

Blockchain technology replaces the need for the bank as third party. Nevertheless, banks can be integrated into the system, because other bank services such as credit or saving plans can also be processed by the banks via Dimo. Dimo is therefore not a competitor to the traditional banking system, but fills a gap in the missing infrastructure. So there is no intermediate third instance, but the blockchain technology ensures security for the parties involved. The idea that blockchain technology makes it possible for parties to act without a third instance and who do not trust each other is therefore fully used here.

In this context, blockchain technology ensures the following for users. (1) Users can receive and send digital central bank money quickly and free of charge using their mobile device. (2) All transactions are traceable and information about them cannot be deleted or changed. Companies also have advantages when using the platform. The platform is connected to the tax office, so that taxes can be calculated and transferred directly. On the one hand, there is no possibility of evading taxes (intentionally or unintentionally), but at the same time companies are helped directly with their accounting. For companies Dimo gives the following advantages. (1) They receive the money digitally, that is safer to use than cash. (2) The taxes are calculated and booked directly from the income, and this is transparent and traceable thanks to the blockchain technology.

Companies can also send money digitally with Dimo. When making purchases from suppliers and paying salaries, they can use the digital version instead of the cash version. This, in turn, has two advantages for all sides thanks to the blockchain technology. First, in terms of salary, the company can clearly prove how much was transferred at what time and the employee can use the digital money immediately and securely. Second, when paying to suppliers or other service providers, the payment is verified by the platform so there is no room for error because the blockchain technology provides proof of all transactions.

At the same time, the information on the income of employees and service providers can also be forwarded to the tax office and taxes can be deducted. Another function serves as evidence: It is also possible to send texts and files, such as a PDF.

In this way, invoices can be sent from one company to the other and the recipient of the invoice can transfer the amount immediately in an answer to the message with the invoice. Dimo can also be integrated by companies into their own online shopping systems, which means that users without a bank account now have the ability to shop online. Investments in companies can be made via Dimo as well. This affects both local companies and startups. Local companies can then be supported through direct transactions and investments can be made in startups, including through institutional investors. The platform also enables aid organizations to transfer money to people in need in a simple and understandable way. It gives the ability to send donations through aid organizations or national grants digitally to institutions such as schools or hospitals. Transparency and traceability are important advantages that arise from blockchain technology. Simple connections between donors in the western world and direct access to the recipients can also be set up via Dimo. For example, people can go to a website for donors looking for aid projects or institutions and send the money directly via Dimo. So, in addition to the direct economic advantages, such as paying for goods and transferring salaries, the platform also helps to solve social problems directly.

5.2.2 Data Analysis

In addition to the advantages in terms of transactions, blockchain technology creates another advantage: The data from these transactions can also be secured and evaluated in a non-falsifiable way, data protection guidelines are strictly adhered to. The data help companies, both local and international, to adapt their products to the real needs of the population. Blockchain Technology ensures the following with regard to data:

- The data cannot be changed and cannot be falsified. It is therefore always safe and therefore trustworthy, even without a third controlling authority such as a notary.
- It can be traced where the data was passed on. Unauthorized or non-transparent disclosure is therefore not possible.

As a purely economic point of view, thanks to the data, products can be optimized and at the same time advertising can be placed more precisely. Local companies can use it to address and retain their potential customers directly. But aid organizations, governments, and institutions can also use the data, for example, by providing targeted digital information based on consumer behavior, the region of the users or their age and gender.

5.3 Conclusion

At Dimo, the advantages of blockchain technology, like the immutable and trace-able, are used to use digital central bank money via mobile devices. It is a good example of how blockchain solutions can solve real problems and also how privately developed solutions can be used by government bodies, as they bring economic and social benefits. From our side, the company Chainsulting, this is just one of several use cases where blockchain technology has been integrated into applications. This shows for us that the technology is not a purely theoretical possibility in the future but has already arrived in the reality of companies and governments today.

References

1. Paik, H.Y., Xu, X., Bandara, H.M.N.D., Lee, S.U., Lo, S.K.: Analysis of data management in blockchain-based systems: From architecture to governance. IEEE Access 7, 186091–186107 (2019). http://dblp.uni-trier.de/db/journals/access/access7.htmlPaikXBLL19
2. Xu, M., Chen, X., Kou, G.: A systematic review of blockchain. Financial Innov. 5(1), 1–14 (2019). https://doi.org/10.1186/s40854-019-0147-z
3. Xu, X., Weber, I., Staples, M.: Architecture for Blockchain Applications. Springer, Berlin (2019). https://doi.org/10.1007/978-3-030-03035-3

Chapter 6
Blockchain Use Cases in Transportation and Logistics

Michael Kuperberg and Sviatoslav Butskyi

Abstract In transportation and logistics, processes often span several companies or business units, e.g., in Supply Chain Management and in Mobility-as-a-Service. Blockchains and Distributed Ledger Technology (DLT) can serve as an enabling layer in these processes, to increase transparency, trust, and accountability. In this chapter, we provide an overview over products and projects employing blockchains in domains such as trade finance, cross-border rail freight, revenue sharing in transit tariff unions, and black boxes for rail vehicles. We show how DLT is used for Self-Sovereign Identities (SSIs), which transfer the control over identity management back to the end user, and which enable a seamless exchange of verifiable credentials across enterprise boundaries. Finally, an overview over blockchain alliances, consortia, and interest groups is provided to showcase the emerging ecosystems and standardization efforts.

6.1 Introduction

In transportation and logistics, processes and business networks usually involve several participants and competitors, e.g., in Supply Chain Management (SCM), cross-border freight and shipping, and in Mobility-as-a-Service (MaaS). Available technologies for B2B data exchange in these domains have evolved from paper-based protocols over phone, fax to email and Internet—but many cross-company processes still use legacy technologies, e.g., because each partner uses an internal (or proprietary) data format, or because standardization of data formats and protocols is lagging behind industry needs. In such cases, different messaging patterns and protocols are used, and each partner decides individually which data to store and how to convert between data formats. Often, the situation is addressed by

M. Kuperberg (✉) · S. Butskyi
DB Systel GmbH, Frankfurt, Germany
e-mail: michael.kuperberg@deutschebahn.com; sviatoslav.butskyi@deutschebahn.com

© The Author(s), under exclusive license to Springer Nature Switzerland AG 2021   61
A. Koschmider, S. Schulte (eds.), *Blockchain and Robotic Process Automation*,
https://doi.org/10.1007/978-3-030-81409-0_6

intermediaries that implement data matching and format conversion—but many companies are reluctant to become dependent on such middlemen.

An alternative to messaging protocols (and to dedicated intermediaries) is provided by Distributed Ledger Technology (DLT): an approach where data is replicated across several nodes, which are owned and operated by different (but cooperating) organizations. The difference between DLT and a conventional distributed database is that a well-defined consensus about each state-changing operation has to be achieved *before* the transaction is persisted; for an in-depth discussion of consensus and its role, see [1]. Blockchain is a type of a DLT where incoming transactions are assembled into blocks, which are concatenated into a chain using hash fingerprints: the concatenation makes post-write tampering prohibitively complex and expensive.

The design and operations of blockchains and DLT lead to increased transparency, trust, and accountability. Thus, when used as an integration technology, blockchains/DLT function as an enabling layer for B2B processes. In this chapter, we provide an overview over selected products and projects employing blockchains in domains such as public transit, SCM, and trade finance. Building on our blockchain experience as part of a major IT provider for a holding offering a wide array of transportations and logistics services, we highlight the opportunities for blockchain technology in cross-border rail freight, revenue sharing in transit tariff unions, and black boxes for rail vehicles.

To highlight the use of DLT in B2C settings, we also describe how DLT is used for Self-Sovereign Identities (SSIs), which transfer the control over identity management back to the end user, and which enable a seamless exchange of verifiable credentials across enterprise boundaries. Finally, an overview over blockchain alliances, consortiums, and interest groups is provided to showcase the emerging ecosystems and standardization efforts.

6.2 Mobility-as-a-Service

Consumers are increasingly booking and paying mobility services over Internet and using mobile apps, with most providers having their individual apps, accounts, and billing channels. In addition to pre-packaged combinations (e.g., flight + rental car), aggregator apps are emerging: they combine the offerings of multiple service providers in one UI, and sometimes even under one end user account. For example, Whim [2] provides different packages which combine buses, bikes, carsharing, and taxis. This increases the comfort of the end users but puts Whim between the service consumer and the service provider—and the latter are aware of the dominance of booking intermediaries which has already led to antitrust rulings in the past [3].

Increasingly, the necessity of the platform approach is recognized not only by service providers, but also by hardware manufacturers: for example, Daimler has a blockchain factory [4] which develops a "Mobility Blockchain Platform," building on Daimler's existing brands such as Mercedes-Benz, ShareNow (carsharing), FreeNow (ridesharing/taxis), and others.

Aggregated mobility offerings are nothing new, and their implementation requires a business consensus and substantial backoffice coordination. This is the case for *tariff unions*, which are set up to simplify multimodal transit journeys: transportation providers often join forces to provide a single ticket that is valid across different services, e.g., trains, subways, buses, ferries, or cable cars.

For example, there are 38 companies [5] in the "Verkehrsverbund Berlin-Brandenburg" tariff union. As only a variety of *unified tickets* are being sold to a passenger by the union, revenue needs to be fairly distributed to all 38 service providers.

This revenue sharing is particularly challenging because in most tariff unions, there is no exact person-specific journey tracking, unlike in air transportation, in reservation-only long distance trains, or in check-in-check-out systems such as the nationwide OV-chipkaart in the Netherlands [6]. Therefore, the specific journey contribution of a given service provider can only be estimated and it can fluctuate even for a given ticket type or zone. In general, revenue sharing in public transportation is a complex backoffice process that includes the following stages: contract negotiations, data survey/analysis, preliminary billing, yearly billing, and final clearing.

Often, tickets are sold on board rather than online or through ticket vending machines, and this incoming money flow is also diverse. Lack of real-time transparency and heterogenous software landscape within these steps and across providers can lead to controversies and additional negotiations, where every organization might have its own estimations. With this complexity and the number of parties involved, the process consumes time and efforts, and the money flow is significantly delayed.

A massive improvement of this scenario would introduce faster revenue sharing (almost real-time), but it would also increase transparency to all tariff union participants—using a technology that is tamper-resistant and which is not under *exclusive* control of a given organization or middleman. One such solution is the Split project [7], which is built on top of the Hyperledger Fabric enterprise-grade blockchain by a partnership of two IT service providers. Split is designed as a flexible platform which can be configured for the diverse needs and ticketing structures of the tariff unions (for example, there are more than 110 tariff unions in Germany, with millions of passengers using them daily, in addition to other major transportation providers—see Fig. 6.1).

Split uses a shared decentralized ledger to ensure neutrality and transparency of the informational exchange. Using the built-in "channels" mechanism of Fabric, Split can create per-need business scopes so that data is shared with relevant participants only, without sacrificing the resiliency and fault tolerance of the underlying consensus mechanism. Ticket sales and revenue sharing are implemented as smart contracts which function as jointly agreed, predefined business rules that run immediately rather than in a periodic, batch-like fashion. It should be noted that Split does not depend on any cryptocurrency and does not implement one, and

Transport and tariff associations in Germany

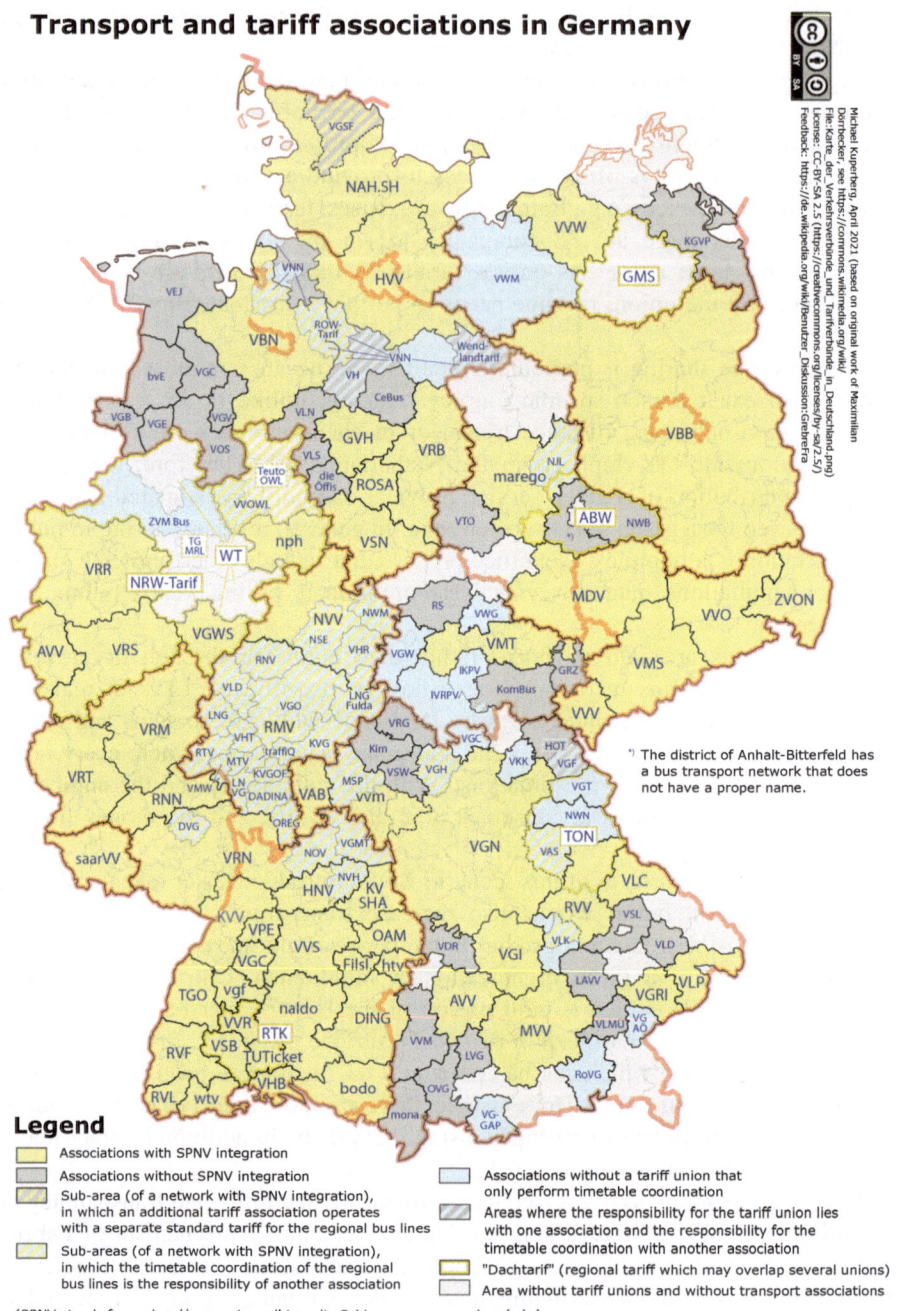

*) The district of Anhalt-Bitterfeld has a bus transport network that does not have a proper name.

Legend

- Associations with SPNV integration
- Associations without SPNV integration
- Sub-area (of a network with SPNV integration), in which an additional tariff association operates with a separate standard tariff for the regional bus lines
- Sub-areas (of a network with SPNV integration), in which the timetable coordination of the regional bus lines is the responsibility of another association
- Associations without a tariff union that only perform timetable coordination
- Areas where the responsibility for the tariff union lies with one association and the responsibility for the timetable coordination with another association
- "Dachtarif" (regional tariff which may overlap several unions)
- Area without tariff unions and without transport associations

(SPNV stands for regional/commuter rail transit: Schienenpersonennahverkehr)

Fig. 6.1 Map of German transport associations, published under Creative Commons CC-BY-SA 2.5 license, based on original work of Maximilian Dörrbecker under CC-BY-SA 2.5: https://commons.wikimedia.org/wiki/File:Karte_der_Verkehrsverbünde_und_Tarifverbünde_in_Deutschland.png

all transfers apply to amounts of fiat money. In the long term, Split can integrate "electronic money" (e.g., [8]) in addition to conventional payment technologies such as debit/credit cards and cash.

Moreover, every transaction is visible and presented in understandable way to all participants, including an end user UI and access to individual transactions. Consequently, full control of the data and service offerings stay with the "joint group" of mobility service providers (which govern and own the system) rather than a centralizing middleman. As the information about a ticket sale is placed onto the shared ledger, it can be easily validated by any participating transportation provider, independently from its sales channel.

Smart contracts allow for further automatization of the processes, such as the rebooking of a ticket for another time and date if plans of a traveler are changed or if the service is canceled. Moreover, aggregation of the service data lays the foundation for the business models that include dynamic bundling, cross-selling, and upselling. The MaaS concept takes the solution a step further. Beyond public transportation, the blockchain-based platform can be used for other services such as hotels, bike rentals, carsharing, etc., where service providers can publish computer-readable details of their offerings to the shared decentralized ledger, visible to all and ready to aggregate.

6.3 Supply Chain Management and Trade Finance

Supply chain and logistics are vital components of our global economy, since they are responsible for the flow of products and services from the moment of creation to the point of consumption. Importantly, SCM also includes coordination and collaboration with channel partners. Complexity of SCM is determined by the number and types of stakeholders involved (e.g., producers, logistics providers, carriers, transport infrastructure providers, retailers, regulators, etc.). They are commonly spatially distributed, have different requirements, work under diverse regulations and legislation frameworks and rely on different tools.

In this context, some frameworks must be established to support common information exchange, to provide governance and trust as well as to ensure efficient collaboration. Thus, SCM provides ample opportunities [9, 10] for application of blockchains and DLT, to leverage characteristics such as neutrality, transparency, immutability, and security. Major companies have started to use blockchain for SCM projects, such as BMW (using PartChain [11]) or Honeywell, which uses GoDirect Trade [12].

For example, TradeLens [13] is a consortium led by IBM and Maersk that aims to develop a common platform for sea-centric SCM. Improved data exchange within the consortium should facilitate better transparency and collaboration between the stakeholders, which include port terminals, ocean carriers, government authorities, inland depots, and intermodal providers. One of the TradeLens components is the development of an electronical bill-of-lading (eBL) to replace the predominant, paper-based version. However, established document formats are very entrenched, as the case study in Sect. 6.3.2 shows (Fig. 6.2).

6.3.1   Trade Finance

A prominent SCM topic is trade finance, which includes products such as Letter-of-Credit, insurance, factoring, etc. Trade finance often involves two banks: one on the seller's side and one on the buyer's side—and the involved banks can vary between transactions that involve the same seller-buyer pair. Over time, tools to ensure efficient collaboration and information exchange between banks and the logistics actors have been developed. Still, the environment is characterized by the lack of trust between participants, data silos, suboptimal standardization, and a considerable number of manual processes. Solutions for vendor-managed inventory (see, e.g., Azhos [14]) may be helpful in certain scenarios, but traditional workflows prevail in most industries.

Multiple blockchain and DLT solutions have emerged to address these issues [15], and one of the largest players in the market is the Marco Polo consortium [16]. It aims to develop a multi-bank, multi-product, multi-jurisdictions platform for the trade finance operations between different (internationally distributed) organizations: one platform for all scenarios and every player. Marco Polo seeks to connect different Enterprise Resource Planning (ERP) systems, banks, and B2B networks to automate and to streamline manual processes, thus providing real-time visibility and transparency to the process. Among others, the platform promises to release trapped working capital and to automate the involved processes, thus providing a substantial ROI.

The Marco Polo platform is developed with the requirements provided directly by the large number of banks and corporates. It is based on the Corda technology and network, where Corda itself is a distributed ledger (yet not a blockchain) that is designed primarily for finance applications and to work in a highly regulated environment. Corda is a product by R3 (a commercial company), while the Corda Network is governed by a foundation [17] with a board of external directors.

6.3.2   Case Study: Railway Bill-of-Lading

As an example from industry, consider the land transport routes between East and West, also commonly known as New Silk Road, and consider the setting of railway cargo transportation from China to Germany. This route includes six different countries (i.e., China, Kazakhstan, Russia, Belarus, Poland, and Germany) and two international agreements/standards for documentation: Agreement on International Goods Transport by Rail (SMGS) and Uniform Rules Concerning the Contract of International Carriage of Goods by Rail (CIM).

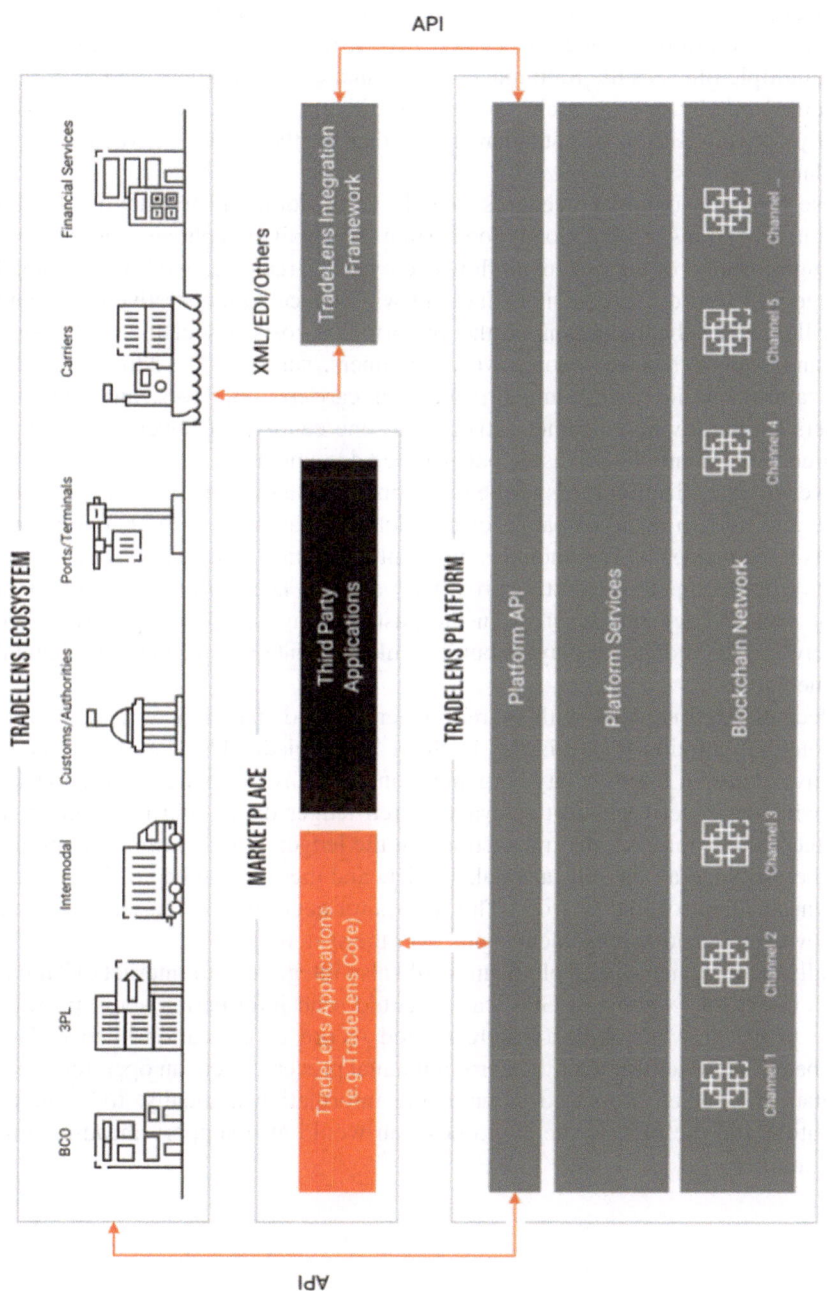

Fig. 6.2 TradeLens solution architecture, (c) TradeLens, used with permission. Source: https://docs.tradelens.com/learn/solution_architecture/

In practice, for every container in a train, there must exist one paper-based consignment note (CIM and/or SMGS, cf. Fig. 6.3) with several paper-based copies; as of August 2020, no digital consignment notes for CIM and/or SMGS are available. Once the paper document is created, it must be verified, stamped, and signed multiple times as the train makes it way and crosses borders (and as copies are retained one-by-one by each border authorities). The documents need to be manually converted from one standard to another (at the border between Belarus and Poland).

These time-consuming procedures include verification and translation; for all the communications, conventional tools such as email, telephone, and fax are used. Digitalization of the document flow and overall streamlining of informational exchange will improve processing time and will reduce administrative costs, and also will lead to the reduction of the opportunity costs associated with using assets and resources (e.g., locomotives, containers, staff, etc.). Additionally, the digitalization will increase competitiveness of carriers, operators, and logistics providers by improving customer satisfaction: one can expect fewer errors when compared to the manual work using paper-based documents.

However, digitalization leads to the questions of data ownership, exchange, and storage, and how to avoid disparate or conflicting data across SCM network participants ("data siloes"). This includes different legislation frameworks, conflicting interests (e.g., competing logistics providers) and the need to ensure a sufficient level of transparency and security. In the past, message exchange patterns were used between the individual players but it resulted in data mismatches and manual adjustments.

A decentralized network with shared ownership and shared governance would be a potential solution to the issues in SCM and logistics [18, 19]. Contrary to alternatives with an intermediary (organization/company) to manage the network, nodes with the exact replica of relevant shared ledger data could be maintained by all the participants. All the transactions on the ledger would be transparent and would be visible to all the relevant stakeholders and there would be no single party that owns and controls the network. This allows for neutrality and easier consensus on the ownership and management rights over the system.

Ideally, a blockchain-based platform would also integrate with Internet of Things (IoT) devices: for example, a GPS tracker could send information about position directly to the network, with a secure trusted record of a location history. This would be an improvement over the current manual process where an operator needs to contact the stakeholders and to enter the information manually. IoT-sourced information and the precise the cargo position would also support ahead-of-time optimization.

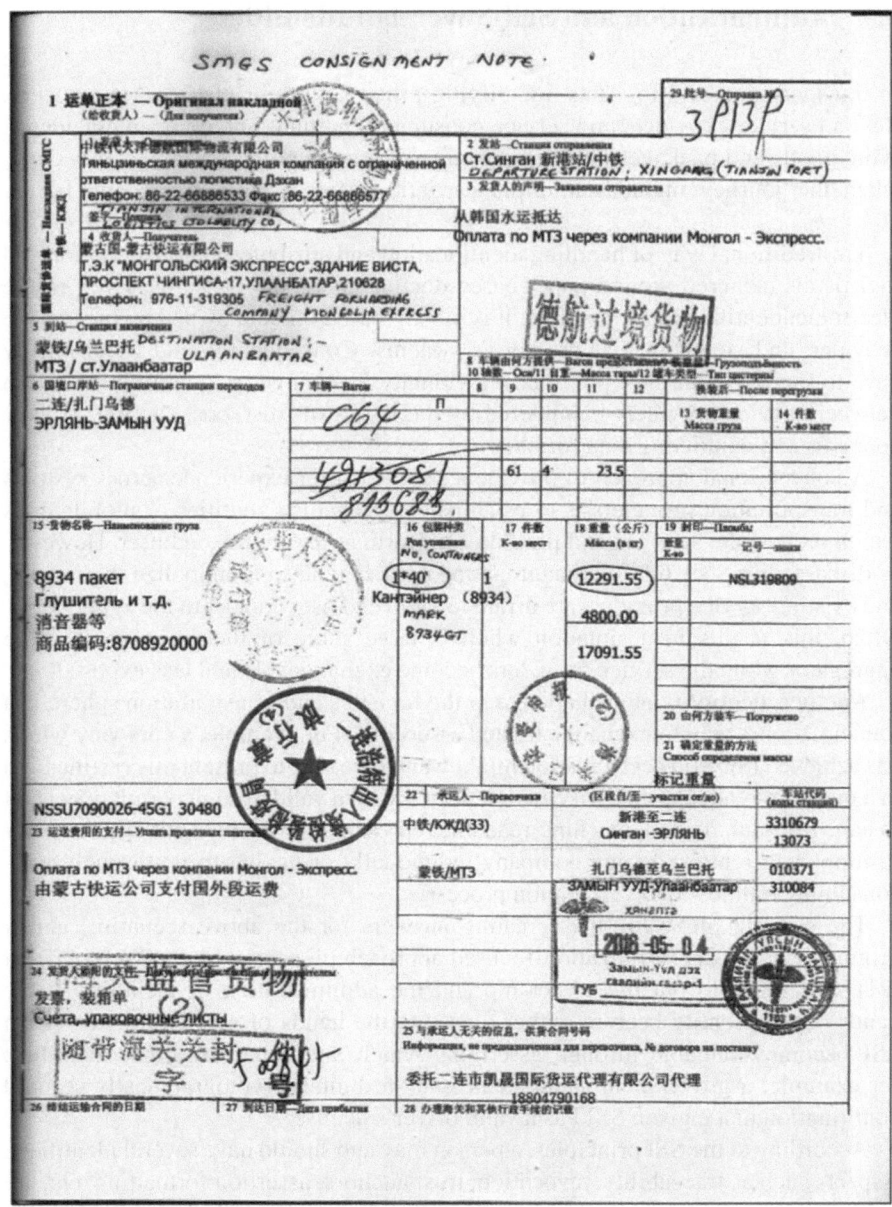

Fig. 6.3 SMGS railway consignment note, as shown in the "Report on Documentation and Procedures for the Development of Seamless Rail-Based Intermodal Transport Services in Northeast and Central Asia," (c) United Nations Economic and Social Commission for Asia and the Pacific, used with permission. Source: https://www.unescap.org/sites/default/files/Report%20on%20docu\discretionary-menta\discretionary-tion%20and%20procedures%20for%20seamless%20intermodal%20transport.pdf

6.4   Authentication and Self-Sovereign Identities

In transportation and logistics, identifying process participants is a key concern. Beyond service providers and service consumers (humans and companies), identifying goods and packages (such as containers) is an ongoing challenge, especially when the journey includes multiple carriers, different legislations, and border crossings.

The traditional way of handling identification and attributes in transportation and logistics is centered around paper-based documents or plastic cards. Even where electronic identification is possible, it is mostly based on data owned by the service provider, and stored in that provider's systems. Consequently, end users mostly have to register with each provider individually. Exchange of identity information between service providers is hindered by the issues of trust, cost sharing, privacy concerns and conflicting data formats.

A conventional approach to provide a seamless user experience across systems and transportation providers is to establish "aggregators": entities or mobile apps which orchestrate services and provide a uniform access to the end user. However, as discussed in Sect. 6.2, such aggregating entities tend to monopolize the market, and existing service providers are afraid to yield end user contact to the aggregators. Often, this results in a situation where a large share of the gains goes to the aggregator while the service providers become exchangeable and less exposed.

Another identity-related challenge in the logistics and transportation sphere is a reliable, secure way to exchange trusted assertions. For example, a company which has achieved ISO 9001 certification might want to be able to present this certification in a machine-readable way. Likewise, a person with a valid driving permit may want to have a digital, trusted, machine-readable representation of this entitlement, rather visiting each rent/carsharing company individually or having to go through time-consuming online video verification processes.

The concept of SSI [20] is creating answers for the above scenarios, and it originates in the decentralization-focused approach pioneered by the Web of Trust [21]. SSI seeks to put the ownership and the administration of identities in the hands of the identity bearers, rather than into the hands of service providers. An SSI becomes valuable through assertions which are issued by other identities: for example, a government agency can issue a digital, cryptographically secured confirmation that a given SSI has a valid driver's license.

According to the SSI principles, a person may and should have several identifiers. Aspects such as traceability, revocation, trust anchors, assertion formatting, etc. are being developed; W3C standards for identifier formatting [22, 23] and verifiable assertions [24] have already been finalized.

Blockchains and DLTs meet SSI at the point where it becomes necessary to record assertions, public keys, etc.—or to record hashes (fingerprints) of such data. DLTs are not a precondition for SSI—but many SSI implementation use a DLT, and the Sovrin network [25] (one of the most mature implementations) is a good example. In Fig. 6.4, Sovrin Foundation's legal framework for regulatory compliance with data protection laws is reproduced.

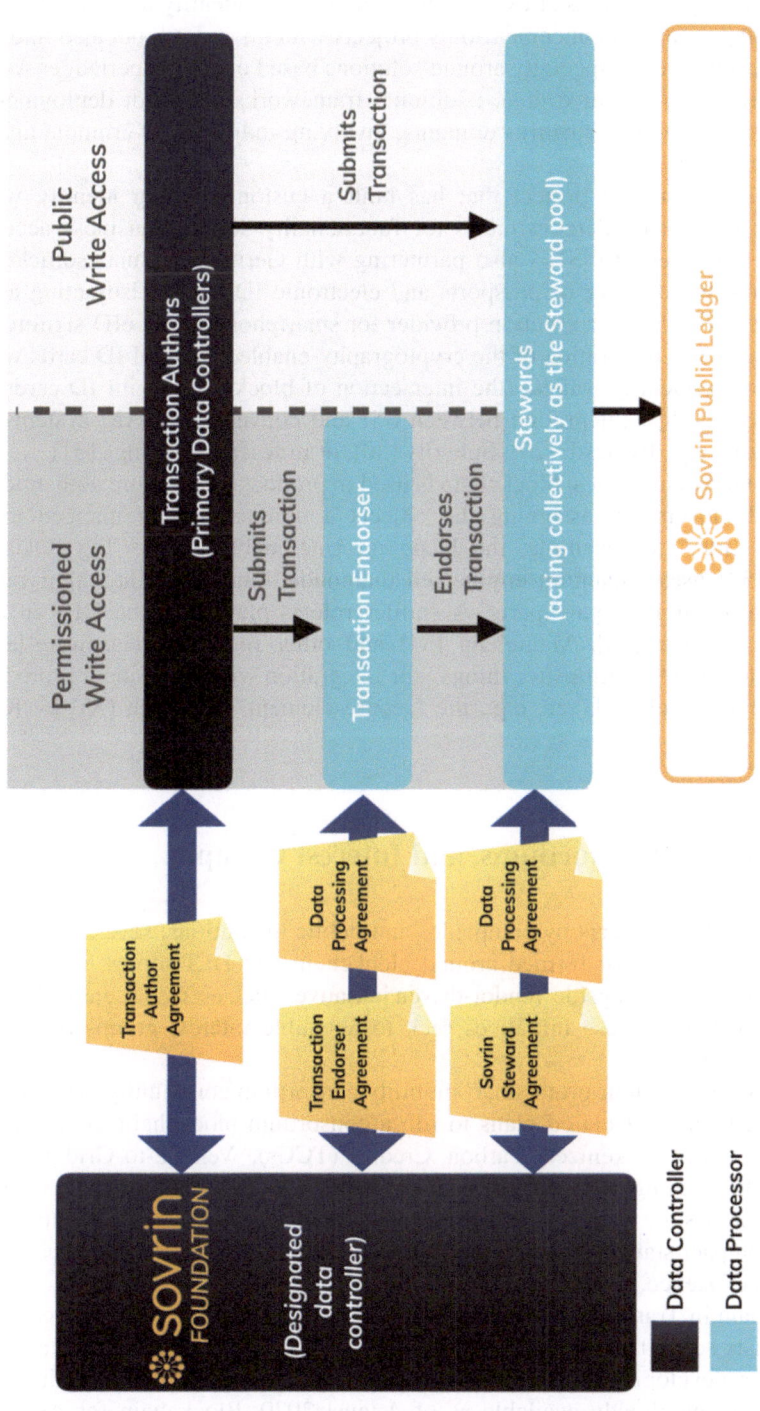

Fig. 6.4 Sovrin Foundation's legal framework for regulatory compliance with data protection laws. (c) Sovrin Foundation, used with permission. Source: https://sovrin.org/data-protection/

A 2019 survey [26] looks at over 40 blockchain-based identity tools and frameworks, finding many announcement-only projects with no updates but also finding intensive development, especially around solutions based on the Hyperledger Aries and Indy frameworks. Since then, additional frameworks and pilot deployments have been started across business domains, involving industry, government agencies, and academia.

LiSSI [27] is such a project that has built a customer-facing identity wallet and the server-side demonstrators for functionality such as business access, mobility services, etc. LiSSI is also partnering with Germany's Bundesdruckerei (government-owned issuer of passports and electronic ID cards, also acting as a certificate authority) and a solution provider for smartphone-based eID signing to provide a seamless integration of the cryptography-enabled national ID cards with SSI and mobile identity wallets (the intersection of blockchains with ID cards is also studied in [28]). Integration between SSI and conventional IAM systems is addressed, too, e.g., by SeLF [29], Spherity [30], or in research settings [31].

Beyond human identities, blockchain is used in products that ensure authenticity of physical objects, by assigning the objects a unique identity mapped to a blockchain entry: for example, the Diamond Unclonable Secure Tag (DUST) approach [32] uses "quantum engineered diamonds" implanted into high-value items, such as aircraft spare parts. A similar role is played by the DLT in the Everledger solution [33], Vaultchain [34] and other registries. Hardware-level solutions targeting "identities for things" for integration with blockchain protocols are also being developed, see, e.g., the "secure element" approach [35] by Riddle&Code.

6.5 Alliances, Consortiums, and Interest Groups

Beyond individual projects by companies and public institutions, several alliances and interest groups have formed around blockchain and DLT topics in logistics and transportation. Alongside vendor-driven initiatives such as TradeLens or Marco Polo (see Sect. 6.3), these initiatives seek to assemble interest groups based on business domains.

Mobi.dlt [36] is a non-profit smart mobility consortium/community launched in April 2018, with no declared plans to run a consortium blockchain. Its declared use cases include Tokenized Carbon Credits (TCCs), Vehicle-to-Grid (V2G), Vehicle-to-Everything (V2X), Fractional Ownership and SCM/provenance scenarios. However, despite the larger number of participating companies, it has published just two compact standards and organized a handful of conferences in the first 2 years of its existence.

Blockchain in Transport Alliance (BiTA) [37] targets good-transporting companies and lists several hundred fee-paying members on its Web page; its mission includes the development of open-source and royalty-free standards, with some initial documents already available as of August 2020. Blockchain for Aviation

(BC4A) [38] has been launched by the Lufthansa, but as of August 2020, its Web page contains only an announcement. IATA has a "Blockchain in Aviation White Paper" [39], which includes the concept of a travel grid, which remains to be implemented.

B3i [40] is a consortium of insurance companies, which have formed a separate but jointly owned stock corporation to seek improvements in the processes underlying cross-company risk management, risk transfer, asset management, and trust/auditability. B3i has achieved production deployments of complex insurance contracts found in the reinsurance market; the first B3i product is the implementation Catastrophe Excess of Loss (Cat XoL) business process. B3i develops infrastructure, protocols, standards, automation, and data matching algorithms; it chose R3 Corda over Hyperledger Fabric (the latter was used in original trials/PoC). On its Web page, B3i states that its customers expect reduced reconciliations of data, faster processes, digital sign-offs and lower overall costs.

As of September 2020, there appears to be no dedicated blockchain alliance or consortium in the areas of railway transportation or shipping, but it should be noted that projects such as TradeLens include these transportation providers as part of the ecosystem.

6.6 Conclusions

Blockchain technology is being actively adopted for revenue projects, from major companies to agile startups—across different domains in transportation and logistics. In this chapter, we have presented different products, projects, and use case studies from a variety of vendors, joint ventures and based on diverse technologies such as Hyperledger Fabric, R3 Corda, and others.

In academia and in industry, further use cases and opportunities are actively being researched. For example, BIMd.sign [41] is a binational research project to improve the Building Information Modeling (BIM) workflows through blockchain-based smart contracts. BIM is a strategic topic for the construction of the infrastructure (roads, rails, airports, ports) which is a prerequisite for efficient transportation and logistics. At the same time, logistics is a major supporting process in construction, and BIM data can be very valuable for logistics providers.

Another example research project is RailChain [42], which is undertaken jointly by academic and industry partners with the aim of developing an open architecture for train On-Board Units (OBUs). In this scenario, DLT is expected to provide tamper-proofness and replication using COTS hardware components, and building on open, established software components. RailChain seeks to reduce the drawbacks associated with proprietary black-box implementations, and its vision includes a better access to the data in the OBUs. Enabling real-time capability through a proper design of the DLT algorithms and structures, but also the suitability of DLT for deployment in resource-constrained environments are two key research objectives of RailChain.

The adoption of blockchain technology benefits from substantial progress on three topics previously regarded as barriers to accepting blockchain beyond cryptocurrencies and use cases in finance/asset management. Blockchain performance is improving, with enterprise-grade implementations such as Hyperledger Fabric capable of achieving 20,000 tps [43]. Blockchain scalability is being addressed by variety of approaches, incl. state channels (cf. [44]), sidechains (cf. [45]) and controlled deletion (cf. [46–51]). Blockchain Platforms-as-a-Service (BCPaaS) offerings lower the complexity of joint operation of multi-company, multi-node, consensus-driven blockchain business networks: for example, major cloud providers such as AWS, Azure, Google, IBM, etc. provide ready-to-use software stacks and preconfigured templates. With an increasing number of trained blockchain developers, we hope that DLT will become stock technology which will benefit transportations, logistics, and other domains.

References

1. Drescher, D.: Blockchain Basics, vol. 276. Springer, Berlin (2017)
2. Whim: All transport in one app. https://whimapp.com
3. Booking.Com Settles EU Cases Over Hotel Pricing Deals. https://news.bloomberglaw.com/tech-and-telecom-law/booking-com-settles-eu-cases-over-hotel-pricing-deals
4. Blockchain at Daimler Mobility. https://www.daimler-mobility.com/en/innovations/blockchain/
5. VBB: About the company. https://www.vbb.de/en/about-us/the-company-vbb
6. OV-Chipkaart. https://www.ov-chipkaart.nl/
7. DB Systel and IBM reinvent mobility by using IBM Blockchain technology. https://www.ibm.com/case-studies/db-systel-and-ibm
8. Cash-on-Ledger. https://cash-on-ledger.com
9. Queiroz, M.M., Fosso Wamba, S.: Blockchain adoption challenges in supply chain: an empirical investigation of the main drivers in India and the USA. Int. J. Inf. Manag. **46**, 70–82 (2019). https://doi.org/10.1016/j.ijinfomgt.2018.11.021. http://www.sciencedirect.com/science/article/pii/S0268401218309447
10. Saberi, S., Kouhizadeh, M., Sarkis, J., Shen, L.: Blockchain technology and its relationships to sustainable supply chain management. Int. J. Prod. Res. **57**(7), 2117–2135 (2019). https://doi.org/10.1080/00207543.2018.1533261
11. BMW Group uses Blockchain to drive supply chain transparency. https://www.press.bmwgroup.com/global/article/detail/T0307164EN/bmw-group-uses-blockchain-to-drive-supply-chain-transparency?language=en
12. Honeywell Is Now Tracking $1 Billion In Boeing Parts On A Blockchain. https://www.forbes.com/sites/michaeldelcastillo/2020/03/07/honeywell-is-now-tracking-1-billion-in-boeing-parts-on-a-blockchain/
13. TradeLens - Digitizing Global Supply Chain Management. https://www.tradelens.com
14. Proof of Existence^{TM} for Supply Chain Finance. https://azhos.io
15. Who's Who? The Consortia and Networks of trade finance revealed. https://www.tradefinanceglobal.com/posts/whos-who-the-consortia-and-networks-of-trade-finance-revealed/
16. Marco Polo - A Trade Finance Initiative. https://www.marcopolo.finance
17. Corda Network Foundation Stichting. https://corda.network/about/contact/

18. Brody, P.: How blockchain is revolutionizing supply chain management. https://www.ey.com/Publication/vwLUAssets/ey-blockchain-and-the-supply-chain-three/$FILE/ey-blockchain-and-the-supply-chain-three.pdf
19. Tönnissen, S., Teuteberg, F.: Analysing the impact of blockchain-technology for operations and supply chain management: an explanatory model drawn from multiple case studies. Int. J. Inf. Manag. **52**, 101953 (2020). https://doi.org/10.1016/j.ijinfomgt.2019.05.009. http://www.sciencedirect.com/science/article/pii/S026840121930101X
20. Preukschat, A., Reed, D.: Self-Sovereign Identity. Manning. https://www.manning.com/books/self-sovereign-identity
21. Caronni, G.: Walking the web of trust. In: Proceedings IEEE 9th International Workshops on Enabling Technologies: Infrastructure for Collaborative Enterprises (WET ICE 2000), pp. 153–158 (2000). https://doi.org/10.1109/ENABL.2000.883720
22. Decentralized Identifiers (DIDs) v0.11. https://w3c-ccg.github.io/did-spec/
23. DID (Decentralized Identifier) Data Model and Generic Syntax 1.0. urlhttps://github.com/WebOfTrustInfo/rebooting-the-web-of-trust-fall2016/blob/master/draft-documents/DID-Spec-Implementers-Draft-01.pdf
24. Verifiable Claims Data Model and Representations. https://www.w3.org/TR/verifiable-claims-data-model/
25. Sovrin. https://sovrin.org/
26. Kuperberg, M.: Blockchain-based identity management: A survey from the enterprise and ecosystem perspective. IEEE Trans. Eng. Manag. **67**, 1–20 (2019). https://doi.org/10.1109/TEM.2019.2926471
27. LiSSI: Let's initiate Self-Sovereign Identity. https://lissi.id
28. Kuperberg, M., Kemper, S., Durak, C.: Blockchain usage for government-issued electronic IDs: A survey. In: Proper, H.A., Stirna, J. (eds.) Advanced Information Systems Engineering Workshops, pp. 155–167. Springer International Publishing, Cham (2019)
29. SeLF by eSatus. https://self-ssi.com/en/
30. Identity and Digital Twins as Trust Layer for the 4th Industrial Revolution. https://spherity.com
31. Grüner, A., Mühle, A., Meinel, C.: An integration architecture to enable service providers for self-sovereign identity. In: 2019 IEEE 18th International Symposium on Network Computing and Applications (NCA), pp. 1–5 (2019). https://doi.org/10.1109/NCA.2019.8935015
32. DUST Identity - Trust in Things. https://dustidentity.com
33. Everledger.io. https://www.everledger.io
34. Vaultchain Gold. https://tradewindmarkets.com/platform/vaultchain-gold/
35. Riddle&Code. https://www.riddleandcode.com
36. MOBI. https://dlt.mobi
37. Blockchain in Transport Alliance. https://www.bita.studio
38. Generating more transparency in aviation with blockchain technology. https://www.lufthansa-industry-solutions.com/de-en/solutions-products/aviation/generating-more-transparency-in-aviation-with-blockchain-technology/
39. Goudarzi, H., Martin, J.I., Meydanli, A.: Blockchain in Aviation Exploring the Fundamentals, Use Cases, and Industry Initiatives. https://www.iata.org/contentassets/2d997082f3c84c7cba001f506edd2c2e/blockchain-in-aviation-white-paper.pdf
40. B3i - The Blockchain Insurance Industry Initiative. https://b3i.tech
41. BIM digital signiert mit Blockchain in der Planungsphase. https://www.industriebau.tuwien.ac.at/forschung/abgeschlossen/bimdsign/
42. RailChain mFUND-Projekt. https://railchain.berlin
43. Gorenflo, C., Lee, S., Golab, L., Keshav, S.: Fastfabric: Scaling hyperledger fabric to 20,000 transactions per second. In: 2019 IEEE International Conference on Blockchain and Cryptocurrency (ICBC), pp. 455–463 (2019). https://doi.org/10.1109/BLOC.2019.8751452
44. Dziembowski, S., Eckey, L., Faust, S., Malinowski, D.: PERUN: Virtual payment channels over cryptographic currencies. IACR Cryptology ePrint Archive **2017**, 635 (2017)

45. Singh, A., Click, K., Parizi, R.M., Zhang, Q., Dehghantanha, A., Choo, K.K.R.: Sidechain technologies in blockchain networks: an examination and state-of-the-art review. J. Netw. Comput. Appl. **149**, 102471 (2020). https://doi.org/10.1016/j.jnca.2019.102471. http://www. sciencedirect.com/science/article/pii/S1084804519303315

46. Derler, D., Samelin, K., Slamanig, D., Striecks, C.: Fine-grained and controlled rewriting in blockchains: chameleon-hashing gone attribute-based. IACR Cryptology ePrint Archive **2019**, 406 (2019)

47. Farshid, S., Reitz, A., Roßbach, P.: Design of a forgetting blockchain: A possible way to accomplish GDPR compatibility. In: Proceedings of the 52nd Hawaii International Conference on System Sciences (2019)

48. Florian, M., Henningsen, S., Beaucamp, S., Scheuermann, B.: Erasing data from blockchain nodes. In: 2019 IEEE European Symposium on Security and Privacy Workshops, pp. 367–376. IEEE, Piscataway (2019)

49. Kuperberg, M.: Towards enabling deletion in append-only blockchains to support data growth management and GDPR Compliance. In: 2020 IEEE International Conference on Blockchain (Blockchain), pp. 393–400 (2020). https://doi.org/10.1109/Blockchain50366.2020.00057

50. Lee, N., Yang, J., Onik, M.M.H., Kim, C.: Modifiable public blockchains using truncated hashing and sidechains. IEEE Access **7**, 173571–173582 (2019). https://doi.org/10.1109/ ACCESS.2019.2956628

51. Puddu, I., Dmitrienko, A., Capkun, S.: μchain: how to forget without hard forks. IACR Cryptology ePrint Archive **2017**, 106 (2017)

Chapter 7
Automatically Identifying Process Automation Candidates Using Natural Language Processing

Han van der Aa and Henrik Leopold

Abstract The general goal of automation is to relieve humans from repetitive and routine-like tasks. The positive effects of automation have been demonstrated in various contexts and range from efficiency gains to the reduction of errors. In this chapter, we focus on the automation of individual tasks in a process using so-called software robots, which is often referred to as Robotic Process Automation (RPA). More specifically, we focus on the task of identifying suitable candidates for such automation efforts. In practice, this identification task is associated with substantial manual effort and, hence, is both time- and cost-intensive. Recognizing these issues, we consider how also the identification of automation candidates itself can be supported through automation. We particularly focus on the way in which Natural Language Processing (NLP) may be employed for this purpose. We show how NLP techniques support the identification of automation candidates in widely used process representations, such as process models and textual process descriptions. As such, we demonstrate how tackling one of the key impediments to the adoption of RPA may be supported in an algorithmic and automated manner.

7.1 Introduction

The goal of *automation* is often described as "*taking the robot out of the human*," i.e., to relieve humans from repetitive and routine-like tasks. The positive effects of automation have been demonstrated in many contexts and range from efficiency

H. van der Aa
Data and Web Science Group, University of Mannheim, Mannheim, Germany
e-mail: han@informatik.uni-mannheim.de

H. Leopold (✉)
Kühne Logistics University, Hamburg, Germany

Hasso Plattner Institute, University of Potsdam, Potsdam, Germany
e-mail: Henrik.Leopold@the-klu.org

© The Author(s), under exclusive license to Springer Nature Switzerland AG 2021
A. Koschmider, S. Schulte (eds.), *Blockchain and Robotic Process Automation*,
https://doi.org/10.1007/978-3-030-81409-0_7

77

gains to the reduction of errors [1]. Therefore, the interest in automating parts or even entire business processes is on the agenda of many organizations.

Taking a business process perspective, automation can be approached from two main angles: workflow automation and RPA. *Workflow automation* is primarily concerned with automating the overall process coordination. This is typically achieved by using Business Process Management Systems (BPMSs) that enable, monitor, and manage the execution of business processes throughout an organization. By contrast, Robotic Process Automation (RPA) focuses on the automation of individual tasks in a process using so-called software robots. Naturally, these two perspectives are complementary: a task that was automated by means of RPA might be easily integrated into a BPMS.

In this chapter, we focus on the second angle, i.e., on the automation of process tasks through RPA. A key question that arises in this context is: *Which process tasks should be automated?* In fact, this has turned out to be a major challenge in automation projects [19]. Intuitively, the suitability of a process task for automation endeavors can be considered from the perspectives of its automation fit and value. Here, *automation fit* is concerned with how easy it is to automate a particular task, while the *automation value* of a task is determined by considering how much time or money can be saved by automating it. A problem, though, is that assessing the automation potential of tasks may come with substantial manual effort and, hence, be both time- and cost-intensive.

To alleviate this problem, we use this chapter to demonstrate how also the identification of automation candidates itself can be supported through automation, thus reducing the required time and effort. Whereas various perspectives can be considered for this, we particularly focus on the way in which Natural Language Processing (NLP) may be employed for this purpose. As visualized in Fig. 7.1, we discuss two manners in which NLP techniques can support business analysts

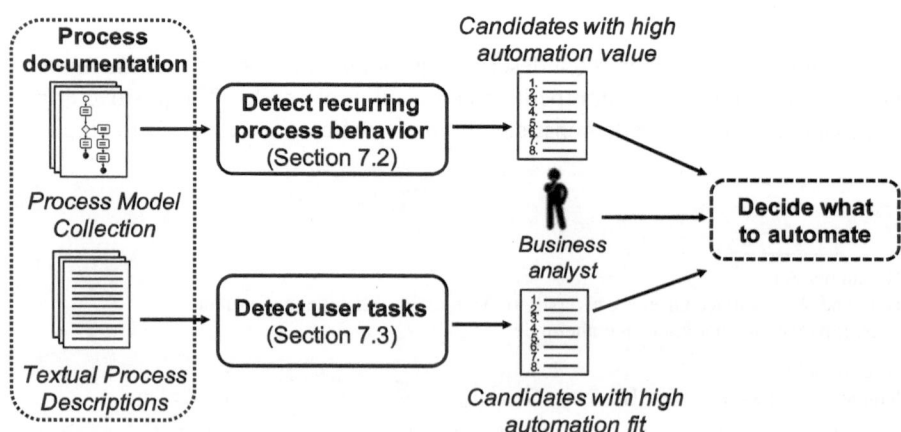

Fig. 7.1 Visualization of the manner in which the discussed approaches support business analysts in the identification of automation candidates

during the identification of automation candidates. Particularly, we consider (1) how natural language-driven analysis of process model collections can be used to detect recurring process behavior, which reveals candidates that have a high automation value, and (2) how textual process descriptions can be analyzed in order to detect so-called user tasks, which are recognized as candidates with a high automation fit.

In the remainder, Sects. 7.2 and 7.3 discuss the general procedures of the two aforementioned approaches to support the identification of RPA candidates using NLP. Then, Sect. 7.4 positions this natural language-driven identification in light of other, complementary works that consider alternative process perspectives for the same purpose. Finally, Sect. 7.5 gives an outlook on what to expect from a technological perspective in the area of process automation in the coming years.

7.2 Identification Based on Process Model Collections

This section shows how natural language-driven techniques can be leveraged to detect automation candidates in process model collections. The presented approach specifically addresses the perspective of *automation value* since it identifies (groups of) activities that commonly recur in an organization and, thus, would benefit more from automation.

7.2.1 Core Idea

Over the last years, many organizations have heavily invested in formally capturing their operations using business process models. As a result, these organizations maintain process model collections often containing hundreds or even thousands of process models. Given the insights that such collections can provide into the operations of an organization, they can serve as a valuable starting point for the identification of automation candidates. This is particularly the case because they highlight activities (or groups thereof) commonly occurring within an organization's processes. Given that the potential automation value of an activity is higher when it occurs more frequently [21], such commonly occurring activities can represent promising automation candidates.

Recognizing this, we propose to employ our earlier work on the detection of frequently occurring activity patterns [14] as a means for the automatic identification of automation candidates. This natural language-driven approach achieves this in the manner described next.

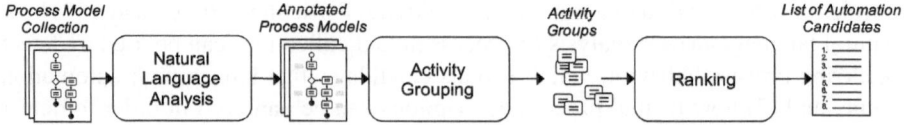

Fig. 7.2 Approach for the identification of automation candidates based on process model collections

7.2.2 Conceptual Approach

As illustrated in Fig. 7.2, the approach comprises three main steps. Given a process model collection, the proposed approach first annotates the natural language labels contained in process models with information on the described actions and business objects. Second, the approach groups together activities that relate to equal or similar actions or business objects. Finally, the approach establishes a ranking of the most commonly occurring activity groups, which serves as a list of candidates that have a high potential automation value.

Natural Language Analysis of Process Models Process models convey a major share of their meaning through the natural language labels associated with elements such as its activities. To identify automation candidates, our approach, therefore, targets the information contained in these labels. In this first step, we set out to annotate process model activity labels with information on the described *actions* and *business objects*. For instance, given a *"Deliver order"* activity, annotations set out to identify the activity's action (*"deliver"*) and the business object to which it is applied (*"order"*).

This annotation task, however, is challenging because process model activity labels are short and barely ever represent proper sentences. As an example, consider the activity label *"Order verification."* From a grammatical point of view, both *"order"* and *"verification"* are nouns. From a semantic perspective, the noun *"verification"* implies the action *"to verify"* and the noun *"order"* represents a business object. For some activities, the appropriate annotation is less clear. As an extreme example, consider the activity label *"Plan data transfer."* Without further context, also a human is not able to derive whether the implied action is *"to plan"* or *"to transfer."* Since standard NLP techniques are not able to address this task, we developed dedicated parsers in prior work [13, 16]. They take process model activity labels as input and automatically recognize the described actions and business objects. This annotation, then, serves as input for the next step.

Activity Grouping Building on the annotated process model labels, we propose different strategies to identify automation candidates:

- *Atomic identification:* This strategy employs the strictest notion to establish activity groups, since it only gathers activities if they share the same action and business object. Given that this assessment is based on the annotations established in the previous step, this strategy still allows for the grouping of activities that described the same activity in distinct manners. This strategy builds on the assumption that frequently occurring activities represent promising automation candidates.

- *Object-based identification:* This strategy abstracts from the identical action and focuses on activity groups that share the same business object. As an example, consider the activities *"Check order"* and *"Approve order."* Since they share a common business object, these (and—if existing—other activities with the business object *"order"*) would be grouped to an object-based automation candidate. The intuition behind this strategy is that the scope of a single automation candidate might not be limited to a single activity and, therefore, may include several related activities.

- *Hierarchy-based identification:* This strategy provides a further abstraction by grouping together activities that relate to business objects that are considered to be in a hierarchical relation, implied by compound nouns. As an example, consider the objects *"order"* and *"purchase order."* Intuitively, one could argue that *"purchase order"* is a specific type of *"order"* and, therefore, activities with these hierarchically related business objects can be grouped together as well.

Finally, each of these strategies can also be transformed from a strategy that only groups activities when terms are fully equal into ones that incorporate semantic similarity considerations. This makes the strategies less strict, since they strive for the identification of similar, rather than equivalent actions or business objects. For example, the atomic-identification strategy would group *"Check order"* and *"Evaluate order"* activities together, because *"check"* and *"evaluate"* are actions that have a high semantic similarity, i.e., that have a similar meaning.

Ranking The final step is the ranking of the identified activity group-based automation candidates. The intuition of the ranking step is that commonly occurring candidates are expected to be relevant than less common ones. Therefore, the automation candidates are ranked based on the number of activity instances they are based on. For candidates derived using the atomic-identification strategy, this is simply the number of occurrences of the considered activity. For candidates derived using the object or hierarchy-based identification strategy that is the number of occurrences of all activities that have been included in the respective group.

The approach's outcome is an ordered list of automation candidates. While this list still needs to be assessed by a domain expert, it provides an effective starting point for RPA efforts, since it reveals process steps whose automation would most likely result in larger gains across an organization.

7.3   Identification Based on Textual Process Descriptions

This section shows how natural language-driven techniques can be leveraged to detect automation candidates in textual process descriptions. The presented approach specifically addresses the perspective of *automation fit* since it analyzes to what extent a particular task is actually automatable.

7.3.1   Core Idea

Next to process models, many organizations also maintain textual process descriptions. The reason is that textual descriptions can be created, read, and understood by virtually everyone since no specific knowledge about a modeling notation is required. Similar as for process model collections, textual process descriptions are a valuable starting point for the identification of automation candidates. Since they often provide a higher level of detail [17], this makes them excellent candidates for determining automation fit.

The core idea of the approach considered here is that it is possible to automatically identify so-called *user tasks* in these textual process descriptions. Such user tasks are defined as process activities in which a human interacts with an IT system, which makes them prime candidates for automation using RPA [4]. The approach presented next identifies these tasks through classification, distinguishing user tasks from manual tasks, i.e., activities that do not involve IT systems, and automated tasks, i.e., activities that do not require human involvement.

7.3.2   Conceptual Approach

Figure 7.3 illustrates the main steps of this approach. Below, we provide a brief technical explanation of each step. For a detailed description of the approach, we ask the interested reader to refer to [15].

Linguistic Preprocessing The goal of the linguistic preprocessing step is to automatically extract verbs, objects, and roles related to tasks described in the textual process description. To accomplish this, we build on a technique that was originally developed for the extraction of process models from natural language text [5]. This technique combines linguistic tools such as the Stanford Parser [9] and VerbNet [18] to, among others, identify verbs, objects, and roles. The advantage

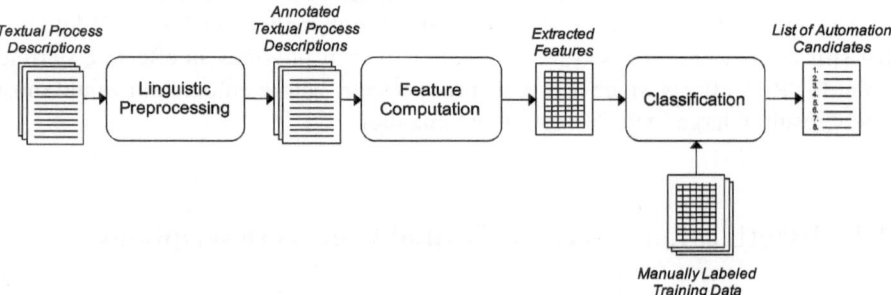

Fig. 7.3 Approach for the identification of automation candidates based on textual process descriptions

of this technique is its high accuracy and its ability to resolve so-called anaphoric references such as *"it"* and *"they."* To illustrate the output of this step, consider the sentence *"The vacations request process starts when an employee submits a vacation request via the ERP system."* From this sentence, we would automatically derive that the only relevant verb is *"submit,"* that this verb relates to the object *"vacation request,"* and that it is executed by the role *"employee."* This annotation serves as input for the next step.

Feature Computation The selection and computation of suitable features is the key task when building a machine learning-based solution. Therefore, we manually analyzed a real-world data set to derive which characteristics determine the automation type of a task. As a result, we selected and implemented four features: (1) *verb feature* (categorical): What verb is used? (2) *object feature* (categorical): What object is used? (3) *resource type* (binary): Is the resource human or not? (4) *IT domain* (binary): Does the task relate to the IT domain?

Classification In the final step of our approach, the actual classification of tasks from process descriptions takes place. As described above, there is not a single feature that independently reveals the task type. It rather depends on the specific context of the task in the process. To be able to still classify unseen tasks, we employ a Support Vector Machine (SVM), a supervised machine learning algorithm. The advantages of SVMs are, among others, that they can deal well with relatively small datasets, they have a low risk of overfitting, and they scale well. Building on SVMs, our approach is able to automatically classify each task identified in the textual process descriptions with reasonable accuracy. As a result, we can automatically obtain a reliable overview of which activities are likely to be automatable.

7.4 Complementary Perspectives to Automation Identification

The previous sections considered the identification of automation candidates via natural language analysis of the labels and descriptions of processes and their activities. This perspective is complementary to existing works that consider the identification of automation candidates from other angles, such as approaches that aim to identify candidates based on recorded event sequences, represented in the form of *event logs*, which capture the execution of business processes [21], or as *interaction logs*, which capture the way in which users employ an information system to perform their tasks [3, 7]. These approaches cover a variety of aspects to identify suitable candidates in terms of automation value and fit.

Automation Value To identify the (potential) automation value of activities, other works primarily consider how often a particular process activity is actually performed [21], arguing that RPA efforts should focus on frequently occurring activities. This view on the automation value of a process activity provides an interesting complement to the approach described in Sect. 7.2. This natural language-driven approach considers the commonality of activities across the processes that exist in an organization, answering the question: *in how many processes does this activity occur?* By contrast, when event logs are available, the analysis of execution frequencies, then, can answer the question: *how often does this activity actually occur within a particular process?* By combining these perspectives, one can thus identify activities that are both common in terms of their presence in various processes and in terms of their execution volume.

Automation Fit The automation fit of activities is analyzed based on various aspects, these aspects cover process perspectives such as time (e.g., execution time [20]), data (e.g., how data is transformed in a step [12]), and resources (e.g., the number of involved actors [10]). However, the most commonly considered indicator of automation fit is the degree of process standardization [21]. Here, standardization can be considered in various ways, for instance, in terms of the determinism of execution in terms of control-flow [3] and data transformations [8, 12], as well as from a process-output perspective, e.g., by looking at the failure rate [2], proneness to human error [6], and outcome predictability [20].

The classification approach described in Sect. 7.3 can be lifted to event logs and, thus, be used alongside the aforementioned approaches. For instance, approaches that determine the degree of standardization may be combined with the natural language-driven recognition of user tasks, allowing for the identification of activities that are both deterministic and involve the interaction of a user with an information system (as opposed to, e.g., fully manual activities). While this latter aspect could also be recognized by approaches that analyze resource involvement, these approaches can only be applied when an event log explicitly captures such characteristics, whereas natural language analysis can be used to overcome this requirement by deriving such information from the labels associated with an event.

7.5   Conclusion and Outlook

In this chapter, we demonstrated the opportunities of using NLP techniques for the identification of automation candidates in business processes. We showed that NLP techniques allow us to exploit widely used artifacts, in the form of process models and textual descriptions, to identify potential automation candidates. These candidate activities are intended as suggestions and, as such, serve as input for a final decision by experts on which of the candidates to actually automate using RPA.

On top of supporting the identification of automation candidates, NLP techniques are also valuable in other aspects of an RPA lifecycle. Particularly, they can also support both the design and execution of automation routines. The *design* of routines is typically concerned with the formalization of the to-be-automated task in the context of a flowchart. NLP techniques, particularly so-called text-to-model transformation techniques [5, 22], can provide valuable support to human designers in this regard. Such techniques are able to transform a textual description of a task into a formal process representation. While post-hoc analysis of the result is still required, these techniques are a helpful starting point for the formal definition of routines. In the context of the *execution* of automation routines, NLP techniques can help to push the boundaries of what can be automated. Here, NLP facilitates the automatic processing of both semi-structured documents, such as invoices, insurance claims, and contracts, as well as unstructured input, such as e-mails, phone calls, and chats. This move towards the automation of non-trivial tasks is widely referred to as *cognitive automation* [11]. It can be expected that NLP and other techniques from the area of artificial intelligence will further contribute to the automation of work. While the boundaries are hard to predict, it is clear that we are getting closer to taking the robot out of the human.

References

1. Aguirre, S., Rodriguez, A.: Automation of a business process using robotic process automation (RPA): A case study. In: Applied Computer Sciences in Engineering, pp. 65–71. Springer, Cham (2017)
2. Beetz, R., Riedl, Y.: Robotic process automation: Developing a multi-criteria evaluation model for the selection of automatable business processes. In: Americas Conference on Information Systems (2019)
3. Bosco, A., Augusto, A., Dumas, M., La Rosa, M., Fortino, G.: Discovering automatable routines from user interaction logs. In: International Conference on Business Process Management, pp. 144–162. Springer, Berlin (2019)
4. Dumas, M., La Rosa, M., Mendling, J., Reijers, H.A., et al.: Fundamentals of Business Process Management, vol. 1. Springer, Berlin (2013)
5. Friedrich, F., Mendling, J., Puhlmann, F.: Process model generation from natural language text. In: Proceedings of the 23rd International Conference on Advanced Information Systems Engineering. Lecture Notes in Computer Science, vol. 6741, pp. 482–496. Springer, Berlin (2011)
6. Ivančić, L., Vugec, D.S., Vukšić, V.B.: Robotic process automation: Systematic literature review. In: International Conference on Business Process Management, pp. 280–295. Springer, Berlin (2019)
7. Jimenez-Ramirez, A., Reijers, H.A., Barba, I., Del Valle, C.: A method to improve the early stages of the robotic process automation lifecycle. In: International Conference on Advanced Information Systems Engineering, pp. 446–461. Springer, Berlin (2019)
8. Jin, Z., Anderson, M.R., Cafarella, M., Jagadish, H.: Foofah: Transforming data by example. In: Proceedings of the 2017 ACM International Conference on Management of Data, pp. 683–698 (2017)
9. Klein, D., Manning, C.D.: Accurate Unlexicalized Parsing. In: 41st Meeting of the Association for Computational Linguistics pp. 423–430 (2003)
10. Kokina, J., Blanchette, S.: Early evidence of digital labor in accounting: Innovation with robotic process automation. Int. J. Accounting Inf. Syst. **35**, 100431 (2019)
11. Lacity, M., Willcocks, L.P.: Robotic Process and Cognitive Automation: The Next Phase. SB Publishing (2018). https://www.amazon.de/Robotic-Process-Cognitive-Automation-Phase/dp/0995682011
12. Leno, V., Dumas, M., La Rosa, M., Maggi, F.M., Polyvyanyy, A.: Automated discovery of data transformations for robotic process automation (2020). Preprint arXiv:2001.01007

13. Leopold, H., Smirnov, S., Mendling, J.: On the refactoring of activity labels in business process models. Inf. Syst. **37**(5), 443–459 (2012)
14. Leopold, H., Pittke, F., Mendling, J.: Automatic service derivation from business process model repositories via semantic technology. J. Syst. Softw. **108**, 134–147 (2015)
15. Leopold, H., van der Aa, H., Reijers, H.A.: Identifying candidate tasks for robotic process automation in textual process descriptions. In: Enterprise, Business-Process and Information Systems Modeling, pp. 67–81. Springer, Berlin (2018)
16. Leopold, H., van der Aa, H., Offenberg, J., Reijers, H.A.: Using hidden Markov models for the accurate linguistic analysis of process model activity labels. Inf. Syst. **83**, 30–39 (2019)
17. Leopold, H., van der Aa, H., Pittke, F., Raffel, M., Mendling, J., Reijers, H.A.: Searching textual and model-based process descriptions based on a unified data format. Softw. Syst. Model. **18**(2), 1179–1194 (2019)
18. Schuler, K.K.: Verbnet: A broad-coverage, comprehensive verb lexicon. Ph.D. Thesis, Philadelphia, PA (2005)
19. Syed, R., Suriadi, S., Adams, M., Bandara, W., Leemans, S.J., Ouyang, C., ter Hofstede, A.H., van de Weerd, I., Wynn, M.T., Reijers, H.A.: Robotic process automation: Contemporary themes and challenges. Comput. Ind. **115**, 103162 (2020)
20. Wanner, J., Hofmann, A., Fischer, M., Imgrund, F., Janiesch, C., Geyer-Klingeberg, J.: Process selection in RPA projects–towards a quantifiable method of decision making. In: International Conference on Information Systems (2019)
21. Wellmann, C., Stierle, M., Dunzer, S., Matzner, M.: A framework to evaluate the viability of robotic process automation for business process activities. In: RPA Forum (2020)
22. van der Aa, H., Di Ciccio, C., Leopold, H., Reijers, H.A.: Extracting declarative process models from natural language. In: International Conference on Advanced Information Systems Engineering, pp. 365–382. Springer, Berlin (2019)